Appreciation of Challenge to Change

"My fourth grader has been involved with Challenge to Change since she was three years old. As she grew up with their program, the skills and lessons she learned at Challenge to Change have become integrated into her system; acting like a map for her body and developing brain to follow. Her default is to literally respond mindfully to situations that arise in her life, rather than react. I frequently find her independently breathing in meditation, entirely unprompted. Her self-awareness and empathy toward others is a dream--the kind every parent wishes their child to possess. At home, our Mindfulness practices have evolved into a shared language that helps keep our family life healthy and bright."

-Kristina Castaneda, Educator, Health Coach, and Musician, Dubuque, Iowa

---

"I see our teachers putting elements of yoga and Mindfulness to practice for themselves and with our students every day. Students are using these skills to help self-regulate and to live happier lives. My staff has been able to change the culture (of the school) into a calmer environment more conducive to learning. This has shown up in multiple academic and behavioral data points which is so rewarding to see."

-Edward Glaser, Principal, Dubuque, Iowa

"As we work to create positive, engaging classrooms for our students, we look for tools, strategies, and lessons that truly support the success of the whole child. I have students doing mudras, writing positive mantras, and doing poses when they need it to help them be their best selves. After a yoga lesson a student said, 'I feel so powerful.' What a testament to the moments that are happening due to the yoga project through Challenge to Change!"

-Meredith Schmechel, Educator, Dubuque, Iowa

"Yoga and Mindfulness changed my life as an adult. I took a children's yoga teacher training through Challenge to Change so that I could give my daughter these skills that I wish I'd had when I was younger. Aurora loves yoga and Mindfulness — whether we are doing partner poses and mantra cards, reading Challenge to Change's Mindfulness books, or meditating together. Her favorite thing to do is practicing mudras. Aurora even started taking an interest in leading me through her own guided meditations and she is only a preschooler. Mindfulness is an amazing gift to give children and I'm so thankful for what I've been able to learn from Challenge to Change — it has transformed our lives in the most beautiful and peaceful way!"

-Tessa Callender, Navy Recruiter, DeWitt, Iowa

GROW

Tending to the Hearts
and Minds of Children
Through the Practice of
Mindfulness

Julie Strittmatter, Melissa Hyde, Molly Schreiber

Dedication Page

This book is for the change-makers.

A change-maker is anyone and everyone who wants to make the world better and brighter than how they found it. Change-makers are forces of good who seek to make truth, love, and kindness a universal human experience.

Change-makers are the people who are inspired by both the beauty and struggles in life. They see, acknowledge, and celebrate all the good that exists in the world; while also honoring the acute aches of living, because they know that it is often only through pain that we grow. But change-makers do not stop there. They use their collection of joy and sorrows in order to teach others and make a positive difference.

The transformation of a change-maker begins internally. They start by acknowledging their true potential and actively take steps toward being the best version of themselves by changing their thoughts, habits, and behaviors for the better. They do this because they know that this self-care makes a positive difference for themselves, as well as for everyone else in their lives.

Once they cultivate a more positive lifestyle for themselves, change-makers bravely and compassionately plant seeds of change for those around them. They utilize their unique gifts and talents to influence matters that are close to their hearts.

We all contain the power to make a difference. We all possess the ability to make a change. May we remember it. May we use it for good.

May we always continue to Grow.

Challenge to Change Inc.

www.challengetochangeinc.com

Cover art and cover layout by Kimber McLaughlin (@ pixelatedpeach)

Formatting and layout by Aeysha Mahmood

Lotus Flower graphic created by Paula Purcell.

Mudra Cards, Mantra Cards, Breathing Shapes and other graphics created by Kari Bahl.

Graphics by Antonio Navarrete, (@johnnythebold)

Ordering Information:

For details, contact grow@challengetochangeinc.com.

Paperback ISBN: 978-1-7363264-2-8

eBook ISBN: 978-1-7363264-3-5

Hardcover ISBN: 978-1-7363264-4-2

First Edition

Contents

The Lotus Flower

The lotus flower is often regarded as a symbol of hope, love, rebirth, and enlightenment. The growth of the lotus offers a perfect analogy for the human experience.

The lotus begins its life by rooting into muddy waters. From here, its stem grows through the dark, reaching towards the sunlight above. Once the flower reaches the surface of the water and sees the light, the lotus blooms to produce a beautiful flower.

This wisdom translates to humans being able to overcome their own personal challenges. It reminds us that even though at times we may feel we are buried in a dark place, there is always hope for us if we move toward the light.

The lotus is also a reminder that beauty can be born from pain, that darkness is followed by light, and that loss brings new beginnings. Everything grows with time. As you read the pages of Grow, watch the lotus bloom alongside your mind as you learn about the transformative power of Mindfulness.

Foreword:
A Challenge to
Change

The Dali Lama once said, *"If every 8-year-old in the world is taught meditation, we will eliminate violence from the world within one generation."*

It is with this sentiment that we welcome you to GROW. This book is an opportunity for you to dive deeply into the practice of Mindfulness so that you can share it with the children in your life. In order to share these practices with others, we must first learn to embrace them ourselves. Therefore, we invite you to grow into the best version of yourself. When we are curators of change in our own lives, we create a positive ripple effect to those around us, especially the children who are deeply influenced by what we say and do.

With this knowledge and the Dali Lama's teachings in mind, Molly Schreiber founded Challenge to Change Inc., a children's yoga studio located in Dubuque, Iowa. Challenge to Change offers lifelong wellness skills that support the mind, body, and spirit of all ages through the practices of fitness, yoga, meditation, and daily Mindfulness. Beyond her role as an entrepreneurial force of goodness in the world, Molly is a mother, educator, wife, yogi, contributor to her community, and trusted friend to all she meets.

Challenge to Change's influence now reaches far beyond the four walls of its physical studio space. It has become an integral part of many children's lives through its widespread Yoga and Mindfulness program.

Like anything beautiful in life, however, there have been growing pains, conflicts, and even heavy turmoil involved throughout each stage of Challenge to Change's development. The very birth of the business of Challenge to Change began with a death in Molly's life. Here is Molly's story and what prompted her own transformative journey of being "Challenged to Change."

Molly's Story

I had what many would consider an ideal childhood. I grew up in a small town with a white picket fence around my house. Our home was filled with love from my parents, two sisters, and one baby brother. I was very involved with everything in my small school and our community.

Once I graduated from high school, I moved to a nearby city to attend college. It was there that I met my first love, Kyle Andersen.

Kyle and I seemed to be perfectly matched with our energetic personalities, fiery red hair, and passion for the field of education. Meeting Kyle was probably the first time I recognized a deep certainty that I was exactly where I was supposed to be, with the person I was meant to be with. Some call it love at first sight.

We married after graduation and continued to pursue our careers in education. Soon, we were blessed with our first baby, Margaret. When I held Maggie for the first time and looked into her deep blue eyes—the same color as her father's—it was my second time of deeply knowing that I was exactly where I needed to be.

When Maggie was eighteen months old, Kyle and I decided we wanted to expand our family. It was then I learned that sometimes when you ask God for something, He answers your prayers and then some. This time He blessed us with two babies—our twins Jacob and Maria. While preparing for the birth of the twins, Kyle and I realized that something in our lives needed to change before their arrival. We decided that we would shift our roles: I would leave my first-grade classroom teaching job to dedicate my time and energy to staying home with our children, and Kyle began exploring career options in school administration.

Kyle became the assistant high school principal in his hometown, which was three hours from our alma mater and my childhood home. A year and a lifetime of change began. I transitioned from being a full-time teacher to being a passionate stay-at-home mom. Kyle began his new administrative role. Together we settled into our new community of Kyle's childhood home.

This was simultaneously one of the busiest and most joyous times of my life. While it was the least amount of sleep I have ever had, and I was mostly out of touch with the outside world, I remember feeling so proud that I could differentiate each child's cry, and knowing that all those long nights and early mornings contributed to building our dream. However, while I was being extremely attentive to each child's and my husband's needs, I was failing to take care of my own. It was the least mindful I'd ever been of my own self-care.

At this time, some friends shared with me that the local YMCA offered two hours of free childcare for anyone who was there exercising. They invited me to join them, and so I started to "work out" as a form of self-care. I would attend a spin class and then savor a cup of coffee afterwards with a friend, or take a fitness class and then enjoy a long, hot, uninterrupted shower in the ladies' locker room.

I began to feel a difference in myself on those days when I took the time to move my body and the other days when I did not. Eventually, I decided to try a yoga class and I was immediately hooked. While I don't remember much about the teacher or the specifics of that first lesson, I do remember lying on my mat and being shown how to really and truly breathe.

I discovered other changes in myself when I stepped off the yoga mat. I found I was not as critical of myself as a mother. I stopped comparing myself to others and could better manage the stress of three children crying simultaneously. The work I was doing on my yoga mat to calm my nervous system was beginning to affect my life outside the studio. I was still unaware, though, how to fully translate these changes into a lifestyle.

Later that year, my little brother was graduating from high school. I decided to take the children back to my hometown for the celebration, while Kyle stayed behind to fulfill his responsibilities as assistant principal. As I tucked my three children into bed at my parents' home that Thursday evening, I vividly remember praying to God and thanking him for all the blessings in my life. Within an hour I was awakened by a phone call reporting that Kyle had been in a serious car accident, and was being air-lifted to a major hospital in Des Moines, Iowa.

As my father and I raced across the two hundred miles to get to Kyle, we received more information about the accident. Kyle had fallen asleep at the wheel less than two hundred yards from our home while returning from a late night at work. The impact had severely torn his aorta, which is normally a fatal injury. However, Kyle's outer layer of his aorta was still intact, which was keeping him alive.

Kyle was scheduled for immediate surgery upon arrival at the hospital, but I was able to speak to him on the phone before he'd been intubated for the flight to Des Moines. I will never forget his words: "I am so sorry. I am really scared. If anything happens to me, take good care of the kids and know that I love you."

When I arrived at the hospital, Kyle was in recovery. He awoke hours later, and when he saw me, his eyes lit up. He was unable to speak, but he squeezed my hand tightly as I spoke with his nurses. The surgery had gone well, but they would have to do another operation in the morning. While the heart surgery had been the priority, they now needed to set the leg he had shattered in the accident.

I sat with him through the night, and again felt deeply connected to my inner knowing and peace as we communicated through blinking our eyes and squeezing each other's hands.

The next morning, Kyle's parents, my dad, my sister and I were able to be with Kyle prior to surgery. We were feeling incredibly hopeful since the surgery for his leg was minor compared to the surgery that he had already survived.

Kyle was wheeled into surgery, and we went to the hospital cafeteria to wait. We were eating breakfast when a nurse rushed in calling our name. She brought us to a room where we were greeted by his doctor. I remember thinking it was odd that the doctor who was supposed to be performing Kyle's surgery was standing in front of me and not in the operating room. The doctor and nurse explained that when they were moving Kyle from his bed to the operating table, his heart rate had dropped and he had coded. Kyle was dead.

I cannot clearly recall the timeline of the events that followed. I was not hysterical; I was numb. I asked for a Bible and for the priest to read with me. I read passages of scripture and the words became mantras. I repeated the words over and over in my mind: "Everything is perfect in its own time," and "Our Heavenly Father knows our needs," trying to make sense of what had happened. Finally I came to a decision. I had two choices: I could pull the covers up over my head and allow myself to be swallowed by the pain, or I could emerge from this tragedy with a purpose. When I got home, I would have three little sets of eyes watching my every move, trying to decide what to do in a world without Daddy. They needed a strong mother and woman.

Acknowledging this, I flung the covers off and never looked back. I hit the ground running and began making decisions about donating Kyle's organs and tissues, arranging for the funeral, and planning my family's future.

I proceeded with life as best I could. I moved back home to be closer to my family, and was offered my old teaching job for the upcoming school year. That first summer, with all its changes, was hard, but I did my best to help my children feel safe and loved.

By the time August and the return-to-school rolled around, though, I started to move into the second stage of grief: Anger. I was furious at the world and barely able to recognize myself due to the exhaustion and misery the anger had etched onto my face. I thought I was hiding the effects of my grief from my children until one evening at dinner Jacob pointed to his sippy cup and said, "Jake's sippy cup," and then gestured to my wine glass and said, "Mommy's sippy cup."

My friends and family agreed—I needed to try and find my happiness again. I recalled how the yoga classes at the YMCA had made me feel, and mentioned this to a close friend. Knowing that, as a single mother, I was pinching every penny, my friend and some other kind souls bought me a pass to a local yoga studio. They even volunteered to watch the children so that I could attend yoga classes.

At this time in my life, these classes offered me even more of a reprieve than they had in the past. While I was practicing yoga, I not only felt calm and connected to my breath, I also felt deeply connected to Kyle. On my mat, I became certain that although his earthly body was gone, his spirit would always be with Maggie, Jacob, Maria and me.

I found a relationship between yoga and my higher power as, through my breath, I connected my mind to my body and to my emotions. When I came off my yoga mat, I felt at peace with who I was and had a clear understanding of who I wanted to be. Ultimately, it was through yoga, therapy, my family, and a really amazing group of girlfriends that I was able to piece myself back together and pursue the happy, healthy life I wanted for myself and my children.

As I healed I reflected on how amazing it was to have a life partner, and I wanted that experience again. After a couple of perfectly nice dates with absolutely no future potential, I was introduced to a wonderful man, Tom. When we met for our first date at the local Dairy Queen, we were both incredibly transparent about our pasts, our goals for the future, and who we each were at our deepest core. It was as if we started building our life together on that first date. We both knew what we wanted and realized we wanted to build that together. We got engaged and married quickly, blending our beautiful families into one. Once again I left the classroom to be at home with our new family.

At first I was completely immersed in being a full-time mom, wife, and friend. This time, however, I was much more mindful of my own self-care. Practicing yoga remained a part of my daily routine. I enrolled in a teacher training course with the goal of becoming a power yoga teacher. Ironically, I emerged from this training not so much fired up to intensify my physical yoga practice, but instead having developed a closer relationship with my breath and meditation.

Something else evolved from this experience. While I had been sitting on my mat in my teacher training, my mind kept returning to the idea of bringing yoga to children.

When I had stepped back into the classroom after Kyle died, I realized how much can change in just a short period of time. For whatever reason, it seemed that my students were now less focused and more reactive, and my coworkers were more stressed and on edge than ever before. Life in the classroom felt frantic and almost something to be endured. For me, the joy that I'd felt when I first started teaching was now missing.

Suddenly, everything started to make sense. Yoga with meditation for self-regulation was the missing link in education. I was seeing a need for more social-emotional care than ever before. I had experienced a traumatic event, and the ensuing grief had fundamentally changed me. It was the gift of yoga that had brought me back to the best version of myself. I thought, "What if I could do this for children, too?" I began to feel my purpose unfold.

I began by teaching yoga at my children's elementary school and in local studios. Word spread and soon I opened my own family yoga studio where both children and parents could experience the gift of Mindfulness. I wasn't ready to stop there, though.

My mission had always been to get into as many classrooms as possible with yoga and meditation. I wanted to reach all children; not just those who had the resources to come to the studio. Working with the local school district, we developed a partnership, making this vision a reality. This is how the Yoga and Mindfulness in the Schools project began.

We started out in four schools, and now three years later, we are involved with more than two hundred. When teaching Mindfulness in the schools, we always tell children that we are our best selves when we, "connect our smart minds to our kind hearts and our calm bodies."

This is an important message for children to hear. They need to know that they have incredible minds and that they are in control of their thinking. We remind them that they have an amazing capacity to care and that being kind—including to themselves—is always the right choice. We also let children know that it is okay to feel all types of feelings, but we have ways to calm our bodies so that strong emotions do not manifest themselves in punching, kicking, hitting, or living an unhealthy lifestyle. We teach children self-love and self-awareness.

Our mission at Challenge to Change has developed because of the love and energy it brings. My own trauma—and my challenge to change—has created a ripple effect of learning, growing, healing, and sharing in the world. I cannot say that I am grateful for Kyle's death, but I know that I would not be doing what I am doing now without that trauma. I am grateful for all who have come into my life and inspired me to help make our world a better place.

I hope my story can be a reminder that the obstacles, traumas, and setbacks in your own life can be your challenge to change. You alone have the ability to determine the direction your life takes. Sometimes it is not about changing your circumstances, but about changing your point of view. No matter what life throws your way, you have the ability to manage your emotional responses, using your energy to inspire compassion for yourself and others. You do not need to experience a great loss to make change for yourself, though. You can do that right here and right now.

It is a challenge to change yourself. It is a challenge to change the world. But the world is so, so worth it; and so are you.

What We Do

Challenge to Change has a vision supported by its mission to bring the practices of yoga, meditation, and Mindfulness to people of all ages. We adhere to the belief that sharing these practices creates positive changes in the world.

We align Challenge to Change's vision and mission by offering a variety of signature programming to support children and those who care for them. Challenge to Change believes that providing Mindfulness tools to children and those who teach them is the best way to serve our world. These practices initially started through our physical yoga studio space.

Our main focus at Challenge to Change, however, has evolved to become our Yoga and Mindfulness in the Schools program. We nurture this program because we believe that schools and those who serve them have the potential to make the largest impact on our world—both present and future. We also believe that the practices of yoga and Mindfulness should be accessible to all children, not just those with the financial means and parental encouragement to practice in a children's yoga studio.

A healthy future directly depends upon children growing up with positive minds, strong bodies, and kind hearts. We believe that investing time, energy, and attention into our school system, both its teachers and its learners, imparts positive change for the future of our world. Our Yoga and Mindfulness in the Schools program offers in-person or virtual thirty-minute yoga lessons to students in their classrooms. These practices are led by certified Challenge to Change children's yoga teachers, and the lessons build in complexity throughout the school year. At the heart of each lesson is an emphasis on Mindfulness and social-emotional well-being.

Our lessons follow a sequential curriculum written by Molly and our team. Each lesson includes five parts of practice that are intentionally designed to increase a mind/body connection, encourage social-emotional growth, and offer a calm space in the middle of the school day. In addition to our monthly lessons, classroom teachers are given the support of our online support center so that they have the option to incorporate additional lessons and activities connected to our mission into their daily instruction.

Challenge to Change further supports educators by providing professional development at our contracted school sites, as well as offering unique continuing education courses that can be taken for teacher licensure renewal. These continuing education courses have been designed with two outcomes in mind.

The first is to provide teachers with a variety of tools and techniques for incorporating Mindfulness into their own lives. This is because when we feel happier and calmer ourselves, we are better able to care for others.

The second outcome is to enable teachers to successfully incorporate Mindfulness into their classroom curriculums in ways that align with their school cultures. When teachers take our courses, we want them to walk away with the fundamental understanding that absolutely anyone who wants to has the ability to effectively teach Mindfulness.

At Challenge to Change, we also believe that empowering individuals to become teachers of Mindfulness sends out a positive ripple effect into our world. This is why we offer various yoga teacher training opportunities through our studio. In order to inspire more change-makers, we offer our signature 95-Hour YTT (yoga teacher training) with an emphasis on early childhood development. This training encourages exploration of one's own inner child, acceptance of our adult selves, and inspiring ways to bring these practices to the wider world. Those who take this training are certified to teach the practices of yoga and Mindfulness to toddlers, kids, and teens.

Our 200-Hour YTT, which certifies its participants to teach the practice of yoga to adults, places an emphasis on adolescent development and on healthy ways to make yoga accessible to adults. This training dives deep into the ancient practices of meditation, anatomy, and yogic philosophy. And finally, our 300-Hour YTT shares deeper and more advanced practices for those already certified in yoga instruction through an emphasis on adult social-emotional development.

The goal of these programs at Challenge to Change is not just to share the positive transformation of Mindfulness with the individual enrolled, but to allow this transformation to positively impact all those whom they come across in life. Those who learn and apply Mindfulness practices for themselves become happier and healthier, and this naturally spreads to others in their lives. By offering a training to one person, the possibilities for continued positive impacts within our homes, communities, and the world are truly endless.

Who We Are

Our team at Challenge to Change is a group of empowered and empathetic change-makers. Like Molly, each one of us has made the conscious decision to overcome obstacles in our lives head-on and with an open heart, leading us to the practices of yoga and Mindfulness. Through these practices we found a deeper connection with ourselves, learned to improve our relationships with others, and discovered more joy in our lives.

Fundamentally, we are normal people who believe in the power of Mindfulness to transform lives for the better. We feel called to share these practices with children in order to empower them to create positive changes in their own lives. Most of us did not discover self-empowerment through Mindfulness until adulthood, but we always wonder: What if we'd been shown these skills earlier?

"I would not change my past because it has made me the person I am today, but I do wonder what my life would have been like if I had learned yoga and Mindfulness skills as a child. I struggled with a negative self-image throughout school and into adulthood. It wasn't until I discovered yoga and Mindfulness that my view of myself started to become more positive. With that shift in self-perspective, I understood that I was put on this earth to help others overcome life's obstacles through the practices that have changed my life. I am so grateful that I have found an organization and a community that allows me to do just that, serve my deepest purpose every single day. "

-Amy Jenkins,
Executive Curriculum Director, Challenge to Change

Each one of us has a deep passion for helping shape both young and old minds alike, and we practice what we teach. Like Molly, some of our team members first fell in love with serving children as classroom teachers in the field of education. Others of us, however, came from professional fields outside of education. What all of us have in common is having made the conscious choice to now educate the hearts of children through the practices of yoga and Mindfulness.

While we are all certified children's yoga teachers, we are also real people going into real classrooms with real children. In these classrooms, the teachers and children are living real lives complete with real meltdowns and real unplanned interruptions throughout the school day. We go into these unpredictable situations not knowing what might happen, but confident that we have something worth sharing.

While we can't control what happens in a classroom when we are bringing the message of Mindfulness, we do know that we can control our personal responses to any chaos that arises. Learning ownership of ourselves and practicing how to respond versus react to situations outside of our control is at the heart of Mindfulness. A guiding principle of our teaching philosophy at Challenge to Change is believing that if we have kept calm in the midst of chaos, we have modeled the most important aspect of Mindfulness that children need to see.

Being perfectly imperfect human beings ourselves, however, there are times when each one of us has panicked or lost our cool in the middle of teaching yoga and Mindfulness to a class. These can also be teachable moments for us if we use these opportunities to practice and model self-forgiveness and grace—also valuable lessons for all children to learn.

Finally, we know that while we can bring yoga and Mindfulness to others, we can't control how much they internalize these teachings. Consequently, when we teach, we are not tied to specific outcomes. We keep in mind what Christopher Willard, noted psychologist and practitioner of Mindfulness, advises those who want to teach: "Teach from the heart because you believe this can help or heal, not because you have expectations or attachments to outcomes." [1]

Our hope is that this book can inspire you to be a change-maker in your own life as well as to those that you serve. Offering these practices does not require extensive training or a degree. Anyone has the ability to share Mindfulness tools if they believe in the beautiful simplicity of its transformative power and possess a willingness to try.

Introduction

We live in a rapidly changing world. The realities of our daily lives are vastly different than they were just ten years ago. Technology, which lies at the center of modern-day life, has created a world that is more closely connected and that moves at a quicker pace than ever before. However, the ability to be in constant communication with others has ironically created disconnection within our personal lives and our relationships with ourselves.

Smart phones have become somewhat of an essential accessory to life in the 21st century regardless of your age. This means that each of us is constantly available, which has proven to have its perks and its pitfalls. On one hand, we might be able to leave the office early to attend our child's soccer game since we can respond to emails from our phones. But in exchange, we end up straddling two important areas of our lives with one foot in the office and the other foot on the soccer field with our child.

While the advances in technology may have increased our ability to be in various places at once, it has decreased our ability to be in one place at a time. Sadly, most of us are accustomed to moving through life in this manner. We multi-task and move from one train of thought to the next with the swipe of a thumb, rarely being fully present for any moment in our lives.

We do not want to discredit the advantages of the world we are living in—information is more accessible, communication is more efficient, and options for entertainment have expanded. There are, however, new stressors that have come hand-in-hand with living in the digital age.

In addition to our obsession with being able to multitask, our society has become more heavily focused on achievement and rewards. As a whole we are engrossed with perfectionism . . . or at least conveying the impression that we have it all together.

Social media platforms are plastered with picture-perfect family photos, adorably prepared sack lunches, gold medals, birthday celebrations fit for magazine covers, and dream vacations. To some degree, we begin to believe that what we see on social media is a depiction of real life, instead of only a snapshot. This causes us to compare our messy behind-the-scenes lives to the polished portrayals we see on the Internet.

It is unclear if social media has been the result of the pressure to live a constant camera-ready life, or if it was the fertilizer that fueled its growth. Regardless of the cause, it is evident that living in this manner can negatively impact our ability to feel content with what we have.

The truth is that while each of us is doing the best we can, not one of us is perfect. Yet we can't seem to stop ourselves from striving for perfection at work, at home, and in our social lives.

To some degree, success in the digital age has become equated with what one can display on the Internet. If we are measuring success by these social standards, we are often left with the feeling we are never doing enough because someone is inevitably doing things bigger and better than we are.

Even though it may appear to be the case, no one is able to perform at a very high level in every area of their life all the time. We need to be very mindful today of the ways we interact with technology so that we don't define our self-worth based on comparisons made with others. While we cannot achieve perfection, we can, however, offer ourselves compassion for where we are while also striving to slowly better ourselves in each moment.

The race to perform, achieve, and succeed is evident everywhere you look; and it appears there is a trickle down effect to the hearts of our children. The pressure we put on ourselves to create the ideal family holiday card is reflected back to our children and fuels their desire to also achieve perfection.

The consistent push from businesses, schools, and sports teams to outperform one another sends the message to our youth that they need to incessantly compare and criticize themselves based upon the performances of others. Furthermore, the need to always be multi-tasking subconsciously tells our children that it is not okay to relax.

These social messages are constantly blasted through the air and into children's minds no matter where they are: at home, at sports practice, or at school. This may be why we are seeing such a large percentage of youth who are learning to form their identities based upon what they can accomplish rather than through investigating their passions and who they really are on the inside.

We see this in young children who are shuffled from one activity to the next, and in teens who are now spending their high school careers building the perfect college resume rather than exploring potential areas of interest through elective courses. In addition, many children and teens who are unable to meet these high demands have simply given up on actively working toward any type of achievement.

We believe this has left many of our children and young adults with a sizable hole in their hearts—and it may be why we are seeing such a steep increase in childhood depression and anxiety. No matter where one falls on this spectrum, it is easy to see how looking outside oneself for value creates undue stress for both children and adults alike.

For better or worse, our world is evolving, and each one of us is doing the best we can to adapt in order to keep up with society's increased urgency and demands. However, as we race to stay one step ahead, we are often looking towards the future and forgetting to stop and enjoy the present moment.

As our world barrels along headfirst, it is essential that we remember to pause and connect to ourselves and to what is important to us, so that we are not simply swept away by new changes and challenges. With awareness, it is possible to stay connected with others while also working towards our individual definition of success. At Challenge to Change, we believe that the key to staying true to ourselves while also keeping pace with the future lies in the ancient practice of Mindfulness.

While we cannot control the world that is moving around us, Mindfulness reminds us we can control how we choose to move through that world, how we approach daily life, how we manage our schedules, how we show up for our families, how we treat others, and how we treat ourselves.

"Mindfulness is a powerful resource that is always readily available to us. When we practice moments of Mindfulness, we gain insight, act with intention, and live more purposeful lives. Personally, practicing Mindfulness takes me from the chaos to the calm in a world that is ever-changing, fast-paced, and technology-focused."

-Dr. Liza Johnson,
Director of Personal Empowerment,
University of Dubuque, IA

That is what we would like to bring to you with this book—real and practical knowledge on how you can practice Mindfulness in order to slow down your busy life. We want to give you a chance to turn down the volume in our loud world and connect to yourself. Mostly, we want you to understand why practicing Mindfulness is important for you and your children.

Life is meant to be more than rushing from one task to the next. It is time to take back your ability to live your life to the fullest extent possible. We want to share how you can find this power for yourself and how you can offer it to others—particularly the children in your life. Mindfulness has the ability to change our homes, our schools, our communities, and our lives if we are up for the challenge.

It's time now to put your phone down, put your feet up, and return back to you.

This is your Challenge to Change.

What Is Mindfulness?

Mindfulness is a term that is thrown around quite often in today's age. It has become a buzzword in society and shared vocabulary among therapists, educators, and yogis alike. But what is Mindfulness?

Mindfulness at its core is making a commitment to be present as often as possible in daily life. Awareness is a generous synonym for Mindfulness because it involves continually observing your physical environment and internal reactions. In his book *Wherever You Go, There You Are*, Jon Kabat-Zin offers, "Mindfulness means paying attention in a particular way: on purpose, in the present moment, and nonjudgmentally." [2] This quote reminds us that Mindfulness is not something that happens by accident. We must consciously choose to live mindfully and can do so in many ways.

Why is all of this importance being placed on Mindfulness? It's because when practiced regularly, Mindfulness has the ability to increase our positive interactions with the world, improve our connections with others, and nurture a better relationship with ourselves.

Take a Mindful Moment.

As you read this, relax the space above your eyebrows. Let your shoulders gently drop down your back and feel your breath move softly in and out of your belly. Congratulations—you just practiced Mindfulness!

Mindfulness is simply paying attention with intention. People often think that Mindfulness practices need to be long and formal in order to be effective, but we often benefit more when we keep it simple. Try and find a moment each day to pause and notice how you are feeling mentally and emotionally.

When we are not deliberately practicing Mindfulness, it is normal for our thoughts to wander. Wandering thoughts will often travel back to the past to ruminate over things that have already taken place. Our thoughts also like to worry about the future in an attempt to exert control over things that have not yet occurred.

While this type of thinking is completely natural, it is important to remember that the past and the future exist only in our minds. Because they no longer or don't yet exist, the past and the future are both places where we have no control. This lack of control can leave us feeling anxious and depressed.

Lao Tzu, a Chinese Philosopher, beautifully said, "If you are depressed you are living in the past. If you are anxious you are living in the future. If you are at peace you are living in the present." [3]

In truth, all that really exists is the present moment, and this is the essence of Mindfulness. When we focus our attention on the present moment, we can alleviate feelings of anxiety and depression. This allows us to be more at ease and live more whole-heartedly in the now— no matter where that is.

"On the way home from the store, my car full of a week's worth of groceries and my daughters in tow, it started to rain. The sprinkling turned to pouring by the time we arrived in our driveway, and I was immediately aggravated thinking about hauling twenty grocery bags and shuffling the girls and all of their things into the house before we all became soaking wet. As I put the car in park and started hustling to fill my arms with plastic bags, the back doors swung open and both girls hopped out of the car. In a rush, I looked back to tell them to make a run for it only to see Briar, just a toddler, standing in stillness with her arms reaching toward the sky and rain pouring down on her. My 7-year-old, Lois, followed standing with her eyes closed as the rain speckled her face. I put the grocery bags down, along with my expectations, and stood in the rain with them. It was like nothing else existed other than the joy that washed over me. Children have a natural ability to live in the moment. Somewhere along the way, we let busyness and stress pull us away from Mindfulness, but children have a unique way of reminding us to remain present if we are willing to pay attention."

-Paula Purcell,
Executive Marketing Director, Challenge to Change

Formal and Informal Mindfulness

There are countless ways to become more mindful, both through formal and informal Mindfulness practices. Formal practices occur when we set aside time to cultivate the skills of intentional awareness, acceptance, and non-judgment. Informal Mindfulness practices, on the other hand, are opportunities for us to apply the insights gained from our formal Mindfulness practice into our daily lives.

Formal Mindfulness practices are singular focused activities intended to bring about heightened awareness of one's surroundings, thoughts, and feelings. Meditation, which is often depicted as sitting in stillness on a yoga mat, is the most commonly recognized type of formal Mindfulness practice. Other formal Mindfulness activities include focused breathing practices, performing a Body Scan, or mindful movement such as the physical practice of yoga poses.

Informal mindfulness practices, on the other hand, invite us to bring awareness on a regular basis into our daily lives. This approach to Mindfulness reminds us that we do not need to set aside specific time to practice Mindfulness. Instead, informal practices ask us to weave Mindfulness into everything we do— from noticing the color and texture of the carrot being cut for dinner, to observing the sensation of the breeze on our skin while walking to our car.

Although it may be beneficial to begin your Mindfulness journey in a designated quiet space, informal Mindfulness practices are an effective way to transform your life in each moment. Through the application of informal practices, Mindfulness becomes a kind of orientation to life. Your Mindfulness practices are meant to travel with you so that you can more easily find peace and whole-hearted living within every moment of your life.

MIND FULL   MINDFUL

A Three-Step Path

People all over the world practice Mindfulness. Just like any other practice, there are many different ways to understand and apply this way of life. At Challenge to Change, we follow and teach a three-step path to Mindfulness. We follow these steps because we have found this method to be the most universally approachable and beneficial.

This three-step path can be done as a formal exercise—such as through an extended meditation practice or in a written journal reflection—or it can be practiced as an informal check-in with yourself. This check-in can take place at any point throughout your day, such as when waiting for your coffee to brew or while driving down the highway.

Three Steps to Mindfulness

1. Grounding to Your Physical Environment

2. Exploring Your Internal Landscape

3. Practicing Non-Judgment

Step One: Grounding to Your Physical Environment

Mindfulness begins by settling into the present moment. Typically, this means bringing your awareness to your physical surroundings—where you are in *both* time and space. Asking yourself external questions, such as the ones below, can help bring you through this first step of Mindfulness.

What time of day is it?

What is the temperature of the room?

What noises do I hear?

Are there people nearby?

What colors are present in my surroundings?

What can I smell?

What is the sensation of my clothing against my skin?

Carefully observe your external environment while asking and answering these questions to yourself. Recognize that no matter where you are and no matter how you feel about your present surroundings, you are in a safe space. When you feel ready, you can move on to Step Two.

Step Two: Exploring Your Internal Landscape

Once you have acclimated yourself to your physical environment, you can begin to observe your inner self. Step Two involves bringing awareness to your thoughts and your feelings.

Prepare yourself by taking one or two deep breaths in and out through the nose in order to further clear your mind and calm your body. Gently probe into what it is you are thinking and feeling in the present moment. You can use the following questions to help bring clarity to what is happening inside yourself:

How is my body feeling physically today?

Am I feeling energized or sluggish?

Do I feel physically strong or unsteady?

Am I hungry or satisfied?

What is the state of my mind today?

Are my thoughts clear or are they muddled?

Am I thinking more positively or negatively?

Is my mind racing or is it focused?

How am I feeling emotionally today?

Do I feel sadness or joy?

Do I feel irritated or calm?

Do I feel lonely or connected?

The answers to these questions often arise subtly, and they cannot be answered by an outside observer—only by you. You might notice that your answers do not fall entirely onto one side of the spectrum, but rather reside somewhere in the middle. That is okay.

Ask yourself as many questions as needed until something rings true for you. Practice the skills of patience and honesty while you explore your internal landscape.

Step 3: Practicing Non-Judgment

Step Three is perhaps the most challenging component of Mindfulness because it has less to do with awareness, and more to do with intentional acceptance of our lives and who we are as individuals. In Step Two, we become aware of our thoughts, our feelings, and our actions. In Step Three, we learn to watch our reactions to our thoughts, feelings, and actions in order to better understand and accept who we are.

Step Three, which focuses on non-judgment, is a practice in Metacognition. Metacognition can be defined as, "learning to think about our thinking." Step Three engages us in Metacognition because it asks us to become aware of our own thinking while simultaneously acknowledging the judgments we hold over ourselves for having those thoughts. It requires that we take a step back and breathe before evaluating why we have engaged in certain behaviors or why we reacted with strong emotions. Being able to notice our thoughts and actions that stem from self-judgment is an important part of becoming more mindful. Moreover, choosing to practice non-judgment is truly Mindfulness in action.

When we start practicing Mindfulness, we increase awareness of ourselves and our lives. This increased awareness can easily lead to labeling our actions, thoughts, feelings, circumstances, and even the people in our lives as *good* or *bad*. We do this without even realizing we are doing so. However, this type of thinking is limiting and lends itself to self-judgment. Increasing our awareness does not require us to implement criticism, even about behaviors we view as less than desirable.

We are human and we certainly have our shortcomings and vices. Non-judgment reminds us that while this may be true, we can most certainly view our flaws and our negative coping strategies with empathy for ourselves. An example of this might be if someone turned to food as a source of comfort during a stressful time. This is a familiar behavior many use to self-soothe when dealing with uncomfortable emotions, challenging transitions, or painful events in life.

Just like engaging in any other vice or unhealthy habit, it is natural to begin to mentally berate oneself after binge-eating. Once a person becomes aware of a potentially self-destructive pattern of behavior they have fallen into, negative self-talk often ensues *"Why did I do that?" "I am such a loser!" "This just proves I am not good enough."* We are all guilty of repeating a bad habit or engaging in something that we knew was unhealthy. We have also all experienced immediately jumping to the conclusion that this means there is something fundamentally wrong with us. Losing ourselves in these thoughts can easily spiral into a web of self-loathing and despair.

Step Three, however, asks us to pause and view the experience from a perspective of empathy and compassion. *Did I engage in the behavior?* Yes. *Is it something I want to do again?* No. *Does having done it mean I am a bad person?* No. *Can I try and move forward and make a different choice next time?* Absolutely. And most importantly, *Can I love myself despite making mistakes?* Yes.

Even if you notice that a behavior you have engaged in is unhealthy for you, beating yourself up over it mentally and emotionally doubles the damage. This is why Mindfulness is about bringing awareness *and* compassion into our lives.

We have the ability to become aware of a thought or behavior pattern, even if it is a negative one, without needing to judge ourselves for having it. Realistically, it is likely that this pattern of behavior has served us in some way in the past. While we may impulsively feel the urge to change the undesirable thought or behavior as soon as possible, practicing non-judgment asks us to compassionately pause with awareness first. This enables us to view both our positive attributes and our shortcomings with compassion as they all make us who we are.

When practicing the step of non-judgment, it can be helpful to ask yourself the following guiding questions:

What judgment am I holding about my thoughts, feelings, or actions?

Which thoughts, feelings, and actions am I labeling as good?

Which thoughts, feelings, and actions am I labeling as bad?

Where do those judgments come from? (Ex: society/family/expectations of self)

What might be holding me back from practicing acceptance of myself?

What bias(es) do I have about myself?

What standards am I holding myself to?

Am I expecting myself to be perfect?

How can I meet myself with compassion in this moment?

Can I offer myself more patience?

Can I offer my thoughts in a more positive manner?

Can I speak to myself in the same way I would speak to a friend?

While acceptance of situations and ourselves is an essential component of Mindfulness, it does not mean giving ourselves permission to repeat unproductive behaviors. Rather, acceptance in Mindfulness gives us insight as to how we can make more positive choices moving forward.

Sometimes we want to bypass Step Three in order to immediately correct our thoughts and behaviors. This happens for a variety of reasons. Perhaps we want to avoid the discomfort of sitting with our unhealthy or unproductive actions for any length of time. Or maybe we recognize how these thoughts are not serving us and we are ready to change them. We may even hold the notion that the quicker we correct these patterns, the sooner they will go away and it will be like they never happened.

Integrating non-judgment into the practice of Mindfulness does not mean that we make excuses for unhealthy habits, unkind behaviors, negative thought patterns, or toxic relationships. Nor does it mean that we hurry to brush them under the rug. Instead, it means that we allow ourselves to increase our awareness with a kind heart rather than a judgmental eye. Awareness and compassion are of equal importance in Mindfulness.

When we come from a place of positivity, we can make kind, helpful, and long-lasting changes. When we skip over the step of acceptance, we are motivated by shame to make change. This makes it likely we'll eventually fall back into negative thoughts and behaviors. Moreover, we are not teaching ourselves to move beyond the cycle of negative self-talk and criticism when processing our thoughts and feelings.

The practice of non-judgment is just that; a practice. It means consciously choosing to accept our whole selves again and again. In doing so, we make peace with the way things are, rather than worrying about how we think they should be.

The Pause

An important component of Mindfulness which gives us the space to reflect on our thoughts is The Pause. The Pause is intentionally giving ourselves a moment to assess our thoughts and feelings before acting in any way.

This is one of the greatest gifts Mindfulness gives us. It teaches us to slow down the fast flow of energy between the body and the brain to assess if our words and actions are best serving ourselves and others.

We live in a fast-paced world, and our minds move even more quickly. Our thoughts can take our emotions from zero to sixty in the blink of an eye, and our instinct is to physically respond to these thoughts and feelings with the same intensity and sense of urgency.

We are so used to acting and thinking simultaneously that we seldom stop to pay attention to how our thoughts, feelings, and actions impact ourselves and the world around us. This can lead to unintentionally behaving in ways that cause harm to ourselves or others.

For example, during a disagreement with a partner, it is easy to become emotionally charged and to act out of anger. Being overridden by such strong emotions might cause us to scream at the other person in an effort to express the magnitude of our feelings.

The Pause asks us to take a moment to acknowledge what is going on inside of us and think about how we can communicate those feelings in a way that aligns with our character. This helps to prevent later regret over our words and actions. Practicing The Pause allows us to effectively communicate with others in a manner that leaves us feeling good about ourselves.

Pausing does not require that we limit our emotions or deny our internal truth. Instead it means consciously choosing to leave careless behaviors behind. When we act with intention, our thoughts and feelings are better received by others and our needs are more easily met.

If we scream or speak spitefully out of anger, our message is lost in all of the noise. It is unlikely that others will be open to hearing what we have to say, and all we will be left with are the overwhelming emotions that sparked the anger in the first place. When we slow down and think about how we can best articulate what we need, we speak our truth with integrity, and others respond accordingly.

"With Mindfulness comes awareness; awareness of your actions and reactions, awareness of your responses to others and the situations that arise in your life. And it is with this awareness that we are able to take more responsibility for the way that we think, act, and speak. We become more thoughtful, empathetic, and more compassionate towards others. Mindfulness teaches us to not only think about ourselves but to also think about other people's needs, wants, and life stories."

-Holly Flood,
Pre-K Teacher and Yoga Instructor, Iowa

Reacting vs Responding

The Pause is a pro-active Mindfulness practice that empowers us to choose our actions with intention. It is where we lovingly observe our thoughts and feelings in order to determine the best course of action to take for ourselves and others. The Pause gives us the space to respond to situations and people with intention rather than to thoughtlessly react.

A reaction is what occurs when we impulsively act from our subconscious mind—the underlying thoughts and feelings we have formed in our brains without even being aware. Screaming, disengaging, and falling into self-destructive behaviors are usually indicators that we are reacting to big thoughts and feelings that have been lurking, unresolved, in our minds. Reactions often happen quickly and are driven by our inherent need to protect ourselves; they are closely linked to our primordial instinct for survival.

A response, on the other hand, unites the conscious and the subconscious mind to carefully consider our choices and potential outcomes before any action is taken. Responses are slow and deliberate decisions that align with our values. They come from a place of empowerment and awareness which allows us to move forward with dignity and confidence in ourselves. Moreover, responses invite empathy into the decision-making process because they take others into consideration. [4]

Practicing the Pause with Others

The Pause not only empowers us to consciously choose our own actions and words, it also enables us to shift the way we engage with others. When we are able to apply The Pause in all of our relationships, we usually find we are able to more effectively communicate and compromise with others.

Oftentimes when we witness negative behaviors in another, it is because that individual is reacting rather than responding. In this situation, our natural instinct is to feel strong emotions and react to the behavior in turn.

This is a destructive pattern where two people's survival instincts are trying to be out heard over the other's. An ongoing cycle of negativity takes place where we react to the initial behavior, they react to our reaction, and we both continue to react in kind. We cannot see or hear the other person and they cannot see or hear us. In this scenario, no productive communication or healing occurs.

However, when we stop to practice The Pause at the onset of this cycle, we are able to take a step back and observe the situation objectively with compassion and insight. Remembering to do this is essential for the times we find ourselves interacting with those who have not yet learned how to practice The Pause.

It is important to note that children do not yet have the capacity to practice The Pause. This is because the part of the brain that processes emotions (the prefrontal cortex) is still in development through a person's early twenties. However, the base of the brain, which feels emotions, is fully developed at birth. This means that children experience the full range of emotions that adults feel, but they don't yet have the capacity to make sense of what they are feeling.

This makes practicing The Pause ourselves fundamental when we are interacting with children. Practicing the Pause with young people gives us space to remember that they are often not in control of themselves when faced with strong feelings. This insight allows us to practice non-judgment and patience so we can effectively help children work through emotional distress.

Moreover, watching us model how to stay calm in the face of life's turbulence is the best way for children to learn this skill themselves. It is only through observing the adults in their lives consistently practice a learned trait like The Pause that children will begin to internalize this important social-emotional skill. [5]

When interacting with adults, it is important to remember that even though they have the cognitive capacity to practice The Pause, many have not been shown how to do so. Keeping this in mind gives us more patience and grace when faced with individuals who do not act with kindness. It also allows us to rationally detach from their actions rather than take them personally. The Pause gives us the ability to objectively view others' negative behaviors as external symptoms of their internal turmoil.

The Pause helps us to distance ourselves and avoid reacting because we understand that their actions are in no way a reflection of our own character and likely have nothing to do with us.

We must stop here for a moment to explicitly state that practicing The Pause does not mean that we tolerate harmful or unkind behaviors from others. Rather, The Pause creates space where we can simultaneously offer someone compassion for their emotional experience while also implementing boundaries that keep us physically and emotionally safe.

Just as the third step of Mindfulness asks us to view ourselves and our shortcomings with compassion, The Pause guides us to do the same thing for others. The challenge for us here is to remember that offering someone compassion also means holding them accountable for their actions. It means loving them too much to allow them to act with anything other than consideration and kindness.

Consequently, when we practice The Pause, we do not make excuses for unhealthy relationships or patterns. The Pause reminds us that we can be both compassionate and assertive while sharing what is acceptable in our lives and what is not. Standing up for ourselves in situations that harm our emotional or physical well-being builds our own self-trust and nurtures our self-esteem.

Our job is to practice The Pause for ourselves and model it for those who have not yet learned to do so. It is not our job to make everyone in our lives live this way or to attempt to practice it for others. Instead, it is our job to take ownership over how we show up in our relationships with others in the world around us.

While compassion and love for others is a part of practicing The Pause, our fundamental responsibility is to ourselves. We serve others best when we consistently model The Pause without the expectation or demand that they practice it too. It is not our job or responsibility to fix others or force our mindset upon them. We only need to honor and stay true to ourselves. We can hold faith that witnessing the positive impacts of The Pause in our lives will guide others towards living more mindfully as well.

"Mindfulness, for me, is the reminder to include punctuation (breath) in overwhelming sentences (feelings). When I am experiencing happy emotions such as joy, excitement, hopefulness AND I remember to take a present mindful breath then I am able to anchor that feeling in my body and enjoy it all the more. Over time my body has learned to trust, treasure and anticipate the sensation of pause.

"Using mindful breath as a tool enables me to navigate challenging feelings with more courage and confidence too. When I am experiencing difficult emotions such as shame, sadness or disappointment, then a moment of pause reminds me to recognise and name the sensation. This practice of orienting myself in my emotional climate helps me to process, land, and release the pressure of my response before externally reacting to the presenting situation."

-Katrina Corner,
Educator and Explorer, UK

Five Mindful Ways to Teach the Pause to Children

It is important to teach children strategies to calm themselves before they ever actually need them. This is because during times of high stress, the brain is unable to take in and apply new information. In other words, it is best to practice The Pause with children using the strategies below when they are already calm so that they can learn to effectively use them when they are in the heat of the moment.

1. **Use a Mind Jar**

   Similar to a snow globe, Mind Jars are containers with a water and glitter mixture inside. These jars can serve as visually pleasing timers that help children take a few moments for themselves. Shake the jar to create a glitter snowstorm. The child can sit or lie comfortably with the jar in front of them. Encourage them to remain there as they watch the contents settle to the bottom. The glitter can even serve as a visual representation of the strong emotions settling inside themselves. More on how to make your own Mind Jar can be found on pages 182 and 183.

2. **Counting Breaths**

   Breathing techniques are incredibly effective in calming the nervous system. However, we rarely focus on our breath patterns because breathing is an automatic body response. Incorporating counting with your breathing can help. Cue children to inhale for a count of three and exhale for a count of three. This will help to regulate the stress response in the body while giving the mind something productive to focus on.

3. **5-4-3-2-1 Awareness Activity**

This activity is calming because it brings awareness to the present moment through the activation of the senses. Prompt children to identify and name five things that they can see, four things they can feel or touch, three things they can hear, two things they can smell, and one thing they can taste, or they are grateful for. Children can note their findings by saying them out loud, thinking them in their minds, or writing them down.

4. **Practice Downward Facing Dog**

Downward Facing Dog (page 215) is a gentle inversion, meaning that during the posture your head is below your heart. This helps to take the person out of their mind and connect with their body more deeply. Since they are upside down it will shift their literal and metaphorical perspective. Other yoga poses can be added onto this pose or it can be practiced in isolation for five to ten breaths.

5. **Drink Cold Water or Play with Ice**

Taking a sip of something cold disrupts the thought patterns in our mind as our body turns its attention to the cool stimulus entering our body. The same is true of playing with ice.

Mindfulness, Meditation, and Yoga

Mindfulness, meditation, and yoga are intrinsically connected. So much so that people are often understandably confused trying to differentiate among the three.

While it is true that yoga, Mindfulness, and meditation are closely related, there are distinct factors that separate each as its own entity. Learning these differences will deepen your understanding of these three unique practices, while also building your appreciation for how each individually acts to support the other two.

Ultimately, one of the best ways to examine the relationship between Mindfulness, yoga, and meditation is to understand that Mindfulness is the overlying practice under which meditation and yoga exist. Think of it this way: when one is engaged in meditation or yoga, one is inherently also practicing Mindfulness. Meditation and yoga are simply two formal ways that one can practice Mindfulness.

It is important to note, however, that these are not the only ways one can experience Mindfulness. Mindfulness can easily be incorporated into daily life in endless ways, both formally and informally. So, rest assured that you can begin to authentically practice Mindfulness in your life without needing to step on a yoga mat or sit in meditation.

While various ways to experience Mindfulness will be explored later in this book, the goal of this chapter is to look in depth at what the practices of meditation and yoga are, as well as to better understand how they complement the practice of Mindfulness. While it is true that neither yoga nor meditation is essential to living a mindful life, there is a reason why both practices have become so closely associated with Mindfulness. In addition to having mental and physical benefits, both meditation and yoga help one live more fully in the present moment and to practice the skills of non-judgment and acceptance—the heart of Mindfulness.

If you have tried meditation or yoga in the past and did not enjoy it, keep in mind that there are various approaches to these practices, and it can take time to find the style that is right for you. Conversely, if you have meditated or done yoga and enjoyed the practice but did not feel transformed in any way, it might be that you were not practicing with a mindset of Mindfulness while engaged in these activities.

This chapter will explore and offer various approaches to meditation and yoga as formal Mindfulness practices in order to help you better understand their intrinsic connection and how they might best fit into your own life.

Meditation

Meditation is engaging in acts that bring about internal peace through awareness. When most people think of meditation, they often picture a person sitting peacefully on a mat with their legs crossed and their eyes closed, seemingly at total peace with a clear mind.

While this is what meditation can sometimes look like on the outside, it is not a reflection of what is likely happening in the mind. Very rarely does one experience a mind completely void of all thoughts, even while engaged in meditation. In fact, the goal of certain styles of meditation is not to clear the mind at all, but rather to calmly observe thoughts as they arise. Quite simply, since there are so many styles and desired outcomes of meditation, there is no single image that can accurately depict this practice in its entirety.

This makes meditation a challenging and abstract concept to grasp. Therefore, if we perhaps begin by explaining what meditation is NOT, it can help paint a clearer picture of what meditation is. Meditation is not zoning-out, cultivating superpowers, or even manipulating the mind. Contrary to popular belief, meditation is not even necessarily about sitting in stillness.

There are many forms of meditation, none of which is better than the other. Some people find one style of meditation that suits them and become dedicated to a lifetime of this practice. Others prefer to explore various types of meditation and integrate them into their Mindfulness practice based on which style is most beneficial to them in the moment.

The type of meditation that resonates with you will depend on what you hope to achieve through meditating. Some meditations are designed to focus a busy mind. Others help provide a path to personal insight and wisdom. Specialized meditations can also assist in calming anxiety and other strong emotions, while others focus on spreading goodwill and kindness. It is important to note, however, that each style of meditation is not exclusive to its outcomes, meaning that a meditation that is designed to bring personal insight can also instill a sense of calm, and vice versa.

The truth of the matter is, regardless of the style of meditation you choose to practice, meditation can bring numerous benefits to your overall health and well-being. Those who regularly practice meditation often find they have improved focus, deeper empathy for themselves and others, stronger emotional resilience, and experience more internal stillness and peace within themselves. [7]

Below are nine types of meditation you might choose to practice. This list is not exhaustive, as there are countless ways that one can meditate. However, these are among the most commonly recognized and practiced forms of meditation in our society today.

Popular Styles of Meditation

Mindfulness Meditation: Mindfulness meditation is a Buddhist tradition that teaches us we can notice the thoughts moving through our minds without judging or physically reacting to them. This form of meditation asks us to practice awareness, concentration, and acceptance of ourselves as we focus on a point within our bodies such as the breath, a physical sensation, or an emotion. [8] [9]

Focus Meditation: Offering a specific reference point to focus one's attention can be especially helpful in a meditation practice. Focus meditations incorporate an external or internal focal point to help individuals remain present throughout the practice. Internal focal points can be following the breath, observing a physical sensation, or identifying emotions. External focal points can be gazing at a lit candle, listening to a song, or counting mala beads. Whether an internal or external focal point is used, the goal of a focus meditation is to keep the mind present on one thing. [9]

Spiritual Meditation: This style of meditation invites participants to connect with something that is greater than themselves. Spiritual meditation often takes on the form of prayer to an individual's higher power such as God, Allah, or simply The Universe itself. [9]

Mantra Meditation: A mantra is a positive word, sound, or phrase. Mantras are used in meditation to help practitioners focus their minds. A mantra can be chanted orally in meditation, or it can be repeated silently in the mind. *"Om"* is a common mantra chanted in traditional meditation practices, as are positive *"I am"* statements such as *"I am calm"* or *"I attract joy and abundance."* Regardless of the mantra chosen, the goal is to build positive energy and a belief in oneself with a focused mind. [9]

Transcendental Meditation: Maharishi Mahesh started the Transcendental Meditation movement in India in the 1950s. Transcendental Meditation utilizes a specified, repetitive, and silent mantra in order to transcend, or go beyond, the surface of your awareness. The teachings of this style of meditation occur in four sessions on consecutive days in one-on-one instruction led by a certified Transcendental Meditation instructor. [8] [9]

Guided Meditation: A guided meditation is when a narrator leads participants on a journey of the mind through visual imagery and sensory details. These meditations are sometimes called guided imagery or guided visualizations. Guided meditations allow participants to mentally visit a physical space in the world like a beach or a mountain through the use of their imagination. These meditations can also help relax the physical body by offering progressive muscle relaxations or body scans. Guided meditations are even used as visualization tools to assist one in achieving a goal. When engaged in a guided meditation, participants are usually asked to sit or lie in stillness with their eyes closed as they listen to their instructor take them on their mindful journey. [8]

Metta Meditation: Metta is the practice of spreading love and kindness. Metta specifically wishes for happiness, good health, and love for ourselves and others. This meditation begins with giving ourselves kind thoughts, as we must each feel love for ourselves before we can give it to others. It then moves on to sending positive thoughts to someone we care for, and then to somebody we struggle to get along with. While there are many different versions of a Metta Meditation, the common phrases used throughout are, *"May I/you be happy, May I/you* *be healthy, May I/you be safe, May I/you be loved."* Metta helps us to feel good about ourselves and to practice the act of forgiveness. [8] [9]

Sound Healing Meditation: A sound healing meditation is when practitioners listen to instruments played at specific tones to target sensation in different areas of the body. Sound healing meditations are based on the ancient practice of using sound vibrations to heal physical and mental ailments. Instruments commonly used in sound healing meditations are singing bowls, windchimes, gongs, and drums. When participating in sound healing meditations, practitioners can expect to feel positive and negative sensations as the guide uses instruments to stimulate and break up different energy flowing through the body. Because this practice involves being immersed in sound, sound healing meditations are also referred to as Sound Baths. [10]

Movement Meditation: While most meditation styles promote stillness, movement meditations ask participants to physically move while practicing more awareness. Movement meditations help to settle a busy mind by bringing focus to how our bodies move and the sensations that arise. Movement meditations are especially effective during times of high stress when sitting in silence feels impossible. There are many ancient types of movement meditation such as yoga, Qigong, and Tai Chi. One can also practice movement meditation through physical activities with repetitive motions such as walking, swimming, running, and rowing. [9]

"I set aside intentional time for Mindfulness practices like meditation, but I also bring them into my day-to-day life. As a teacher in a Title 1 elementary school, my energy is pulled in many directions at once. Mantra meditation practices help me stay calm and focus on my tasks. For me, mantras are a crucial part of my Mindfulness practice because they produce positive self-talk. My favorite mantra is 'I am joyful.' It reminds me to be the best version of myself even in my most challenging moments."

-Kevin Turner,
Educator, Iowa

Meditation and You

No matter the form it takes, what is universal about meditation is that it is setting aside time to observe one's inner world through sustained concentration. In meditation, we withdraw our senses in some way so that we can exclusively focus on what is happening inside of us.

Regardless of which styles of meditation you integrate into your Mindfulness journey, always remember that there is no right or wrong way to meditate. It will be important for you to explore various styles of meditation that align with your personal growth and create a routine for yourself to support your practice.

While dedication to a daily practice offers the most potential benefit, please be aware that your day-to-day experiences in meditation will vary. Some days you will feel calm, focused, and in touch with yourself during your practice. On other days it will seem like your mind was entirely consumed with upcoming tasks and to-dos.

Don't lose heart. All this is a part of the process. The important thing is you do your best to stay consistent. It is through dedication and regularity that you build up the muscles of your mind. Begin by devoting a few minutes each day to your meditation practice, then gradually increase its duration according to your comfort level.

Keep in mind that there is no prescribed amount of time one must dedicate to a meditation practice in order for it to be effective. Some styles of meditation ask participants to pause for only a few breaths, while others ask for continued attention for minutes to hours.

All that is important in meditation is that one enters these practices with an open mind. This means being willing to leave behind any fixed notions of what meditation should look like or what its outcomes should be so that you can authentically show up for and benefit from your practice.

Through meditation we find peace because we settle into our bodies and allow ourselves to be fully present in the here and now. This is part of the process of learning to listen to your thoughts without judgment or a call to action. It is this dedication to the present moment and to non-judgment that makes meditation an act of Mindfulness.

Yoga

Yoga is often seen as a physical practice, but it is so much more than that. Yoga is a mindful movement that increases your connection with yourself on a physical, mental, emotional, and spiritual level.

Yoga classes typically offer physical poses that help to stretch, strengthen, and balance the body while also providing instruction on how to lie still and breathe. At its core, yoga is intentionally trying to unite two things within ourselves. In a yoga class, this union most commonly refers to linking the physical movement of the body with the inhales and exhales of the breath.

While the union of the breath and body are at the root of a physical yoga practice, what can be united through yoga runs much broader and deeper than this. In actuality, yoga is understanding or creating a connection between any two things in one's life. This connection could be between the mind and the heart, the relationship between one's physical body and one's soul, or the intricate connections that exist between yourself and the universe.

The term yoga itself comes from the Sanskrit root *yuj* which means "to yoke" or "unite." Due to its ancient origins in Northern India, the yogic philosophies were first spoken and written in Sanskrit, an ancient Indo-Aryan language. Like Latin, this is now considered a dead language, but it is still presently used in yoga classes and when discussing yogic philosophy. In this way, Sanskrit is a bridge connecting yoga's ancient past with its evolved presence in society today.

While nobody knows the exact date yoga began, it is believed that yoga has its origins around 5,000-8,000 years ago. Like many other spiritual practices, yoga was created as people tried to understand the meaning of life. This quest led to yogic philosophy—how best to live a life of fulfillment and joy.

To this purpose, yoga manifested as an eight-limbed practice, one of which is the physical poses and movement of yoga commonly recognized today. This formal yoga practice, known as *asana* in Sanskrit, typically takes place over the course of an hour where an instructor cues physical poses with matching breaths. *Asana* has always played an important role in yoga because ancient *yogis* have long understood what modern scientists are just recently beginning to understand—that human beings benefit more from meditative practices after they have first engaged in some form of physical activity.

Thus, the main goal of a yoga practice is not to be able to touch your toes or stand on your head, but for individuals to burn off excess energy so that they can arrive at a place of mental clarity. It is through learning to sit with oneself, breathe in challenging postures, and being mentally flexible when presented with change and novelty that your yoga mat can become more than a home for your physical practice. It can also offer a safe space to examine how we can apply truths and lessons from yogic philosophy within our daily lives.

While *asana* might be what is most commonly associated with yoga today, the other seven limbs are equally as important in understanding the power of yoga as a whole. Each limb holds an important truth towards living a life of fulfillment and value.

The Eight Limbs of Yoga

1. **Yamas:** These are the ethical standards for living life with integrity. These standards include nonviolence, truthfulness, non-stealing, continence (self-restraint), and non-covetousness.

2. **Niyamas:** This is the practice of self-discipline with the spiritual observances of purification and cleanliness, contentment with and appreciation for what one has, willpower, self-study and self-reflection, and surrender to a higher power than oneself.

3. **Asana:** The physical practice of moving the body using yoga poses.

4. **Pranayama:** Mastery of the breath through certain techniques and exercises.

5. **Pratyahara:** Withdrawal of the senses for the purpose of self-observation.

6. **Dharana:** Focused attention of the mind on a single point.

7. **Dhyana:** The uninterrupted flow of concentration within oneself (Meditation).

8. **Samadhi:** A state of ecstasy or connection to the Divine.

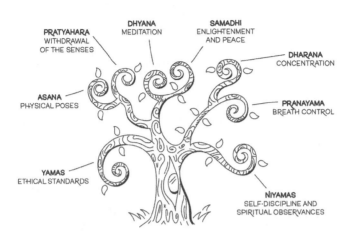

Much like that of a tree in nature, the branches of yoga stem from the same roots, but each reaches separately in its own direction to create a structure that is complex, beautiful, and whole. The understanding of the limbs in union offers a richer understanding of the transformative powers of yoga on and off of the mat.

Today, yoga is widely accepted and practiced globally. While some practitioners choose to dive deep into yogic philosophy, others choose to dedicate themselves more heavily to their physical yoga practice. There is no right or wrong way to explore yoga in your life. If nothing else, allow these eight limbs to serve as a reminder that yoga is not just about your physical prowess, but is a means towards understanding and nurturing yourself more deeply.

What you will take out of your yoga practice is unique to you as an individual. Remember that yoga is about union and connection. It is up to each practitioner to determine the intention of their practice; in other words, what it is they wish to unite within themselves. Perhaps the intention is a union of the body and the mind through focused breathing and intentional movement, the union of the body and the spirit through deep meditation and surrender, or the union of self to others through compassionate awareness. Yoga is your invitation to move closer to your truest self.

"A lot of people come to yoga for the physical aspect— to increase flexibility, build strength, and tone their bodies. Honestly, I did too. In the beginning, participants focus so much on the names of the poses and getting the anatomical cues right. But once the poses become more familiar and we figure out what the teacher is saying, we move beyond the physical component, we are free to explore the depth and calm that come with practice. I call this the secondary benefit—but I actually believe it is the primary benefit of yoga. It is almost impossible to practice the physical poses without experiencing the other limbs of yoga. The irony of yoga is that most people come to practice for physical rewards, but they leave with more internal strength, mental flexibility, and inner peace."

-Mae Hingtgen,
Social Worker and Yoga Instructor, Iowa

"Sometimes quieting our minds helps us to quiet our bodies; sometimes we must quiet our bodies first before we can find the way to a really quiet mind . . . Each individual must judge for herself as to the best way of reaching the quiet."

-Annie Payson Call, *Nerves and Common Sense* [11]

Many Ways to Practice

As previously mentioned, yoga not only supports a healthy physical body, but it also opens up space in the mind for deep internal reflection. The way in which one arrives at this state of mental clarity is different from person to person and, within each person, can change day-to-day. Sometimes we find peace more easily after vigorous movement, while at other times we strongly benefit from a meditative class rooted in stillness. Regardless of the structure and intensity of a yoga practice, the destination is the same—authentic and intentional internal reflection.

There are endless styles in which *asana* is practiced today, and within each style, new interpretations and themes are constantly emerging. Some styles of yoga are rooted in ancient tradition, remaining true to its original teachings and techniques. Many other forms of yoga, however, have been adapted and specialized for certain demographics or for specific intended outcomes.

While the list below is not an exhaustive explanation of the ways in which one can engage in a physical yoga practice, it does provide a description of many of the types of yoga classes available today.

Popular Styles of Yoga:

Hatha Yoga: The Sanskrit term *Hatha* most closely translates to "effort" or "force". This style of yoga is often recognized for its ability to balance the energetic body; specifically, the masculine and feminine energies that we all contain. It can also be looked at as the balance of the solar and lunar energy within ourselves. This translates to finding effort paired with ease and strength matched with surrender. Traditionally, Hatha Yoga classes offer a slow to moderately paced flow that combines poses, breathing exercises, and meditation. Therefore, various styles of yoga can fall under the umbrella of *Hatha*. It is best to ask your yoga teacher what you can anticipate from their interpretation of a Hatha Yoga practice. [12]

Ashtanga Yoga: This is an incredibly physical flow-based style of yoga. Ashtanga Yoga classes follow a specific sequential order that offers the same six series of poses. The series build in complexity as they progress; each requiring more strength and flexibility than the last. Ashtanga Yoga follows the ancient tradition of students beginning with Series One, The Primary Series of poses, and moving on to the Intermediate Series once their instructor has deemed they are ready. If you were to visit a yoga studio offering traditional Ashtanga Yoga, you would see students in various poses at different times. This is because each student is instructed to follow their sequence at the pace of their own breath. One of the greatest benefits of Ashtanga Yoga is that it offers a great deal of structure in its sequences yet allows for individual freedom to explore a personal edge within each pose. In the United States, however, Ashtanga Yoga has evolved to often being led as a guided practice, in which a yoga teacher leads the class through Series One or Series Two over the course of seventy-five or ninety minutes. [12]

Vinyasa Yoga: Vinyasa Yoga is typically an energetic practice that links movement to breath. In a Vinyasa style practice, the breath is used as a guide for when to move from pose to pose. Usually movements away from the earth are cued with an inhale, while poses that bring you closer to the floor are paired with an exhale. The translation of the Sanskrit word *Vinyasa* is "to place in a special way", which connects to how participants mindfully flow throughout the class. This style of yoga places great emphasis on moving the spine in all directions. Therefore, teachers deliberately create sequences to strengthen, stretch, and open various areas of the body while offering alignment and breath cues. Unlike many other styles of yoga, Vinyasa does not just focus on isolated poses. Instead, these classes place equal emphasis on how one flows from one pose to the next, reminding us that transitions are just as important as the destination. [12]

Power Yoga: Power Yoga is heavily recognized for its athletic component and is incredibly popular in yoga studios as well as fitness centers. Power Yoga offers a vigorous approach to Vinyasa Yoga and is also a derivative of Ashtanga Yoga. This fast-paced practice combines the benefits of aerobic exercise, strength training, and traditional yoga as it increases the heart rate, builds muscle, and improves flexibility. These classes are offered in both hot studios and non-heated spaces. Baptiste Yoga, created by Baron Baptiste, is a widely practiced interpretation of Power Yoga. [12]

Kundalini Yoga: Kundalini Yoga gets its name from the Sanskrit word *kundal*, which translates to "circular" or "snake". Kundalini Yoga is based on the belief that everyone has a powerful life force energy sitting in a coiled shape at the base of the spine. Kundalini Yoga seeks to release this energy and move it upwards through the body in order to help individuals reach Enlightenment. In a Kundalini practice, participants are led through chanting, singing, focused breath practices, and repeated physical movements to stimulate and move this life energy force upward through the physical body and energetic channels. Traditional yoga poses may or may not be incorporated into a Kundalini class. [12]

Yin Yoga: Yin Yoga is a slow-paced practice in which participants hold poses for extended periods of time. Yin Yoga is a great compliment to faster paced styles of yoga, such as Power or Vinyasa Yoga, which focus primarily on stretching the outer muscles of the body through intense physical movement. Yin Yoga gets its name from the two types of energy, Yin and Yang. Yin is the energy that cools and soothes to balance out the fire and heat of Yang. In a Yin Yoga class, you might experience the same poses as a Yang style practice. However, the names of the poses and the cues to settle into these poses will vary slightly as their intended outcomes are different. Yang Yoga seeks to stretch the muscles, while Yin Yoga focuses on relaxing the muscles in order to release energy from the deeper tissue, such as the fascia, joints, and ligaments. Yin Yoga participants are guided to turn inward and reflect as they hold each pose for two to five minutes. [13]

Restorative Yoga: The goal of Restorative Yoga is to renew and revive. It seeks to restore physical and emotional well-being through relaxing poses and calming meditation. This form of yoga generally only incorporates seated or lying down postures that are then modified for ease through the use of props such as bolsters, blankets, and blocks. Similar to Yin Yoga, only a few poses are practiced during a Restorative Yoga class because each pose is held for five minutes or longer. Unlike Yin Yoga where physical discomfort is welcomed to release tension, Restorative Yoga relies heavily on the use of props to make the body as comfortable as possible as it settles into each pose. The combination of support from props and extended time in each pose offers the body and mind ample time to relax and release tension. [13]

Prenatal and Postnatal Yoga: These classes are tailored for soon-to-be mothers and women postpartum. Because not all yoga poses are suitable during and immediately following pregnancy, Prenatal and Postnatal Yoga offer modifications that keep new and expectant moms' changing bodies safe and strong. These styles of yoga are a great way to maintain physical health, ease back into exercise, and manage the stress that arises from such a major life change. Despite the classes being designed for prepartum and postpartum women, please check with a medical professional before participating in one of these classes. [12]

Children's Yoga: Children's yoga classes introduce infants, toddlers, school-age children, and teens to yoga practices and traditions. They are designed to engage youth through developmentally appropriate physical and meditative practices, and often incorporate storytelling, songs, and games.

AcroYoga: AcroYoga is a combination of traditional Hatha or Vinyasa Yoga with acrobatics. It usually involves partner or group practices in which individuals are lifted into the air by their partner or the group. It is a rigorous practice that uses gravity to strengthen and stretch its participants. Elements of Thai massage are often incorporated at the close of practice to further enhance this practice's health benefits. [14]

Aerial Yoga: Aerial Yoga uses a hammock or a swing which participants interact with throughout the class. At times the swing is more of a prop to support a pose on the ground, while at other times, students can practice a yoga pose while standing or sitting in the swing. Like any other prop, the hammocks or swings assist participants in deepening their practice and can make yoga poses they might not be able to achieve on the ground accessible. Elements of dance and Pilates are often incorporated into a typical Aerial Yoga class. Because the practice takes place primarily in the air, Aerial Yoga is also called Antigravity Yoga. [14]

Savasana

At its heart, yoga was, and still is, a tradition centered around finding the path to enlightenment and one's true self. You will find this to be true no matter which style of yoga you choose to explore. Because of this, there are some commonalities you will find across every type of yoga class—the most important of which is probably *Savasana*.

In order to ensure that a portion of class is centered around internal reflection, yoga instructors intentionally create space at the end of a yoga practice for meditation. This is referred to as *Savasana* or final relaxation. During this time participants lie on their backs in stillness with their legs stretched long and their arms at their sides. Despite Savasana having little physical exertion associated with it, it is often the most mentally challenging part of class for most individuals, as we are very rarely asked to slow down in our busy world.

This stillness at the end of class is important because it allows *yogis,* or those who practice yoga, to listen to their thoughts and feelings while working towards internal peace. And this is the ultimate reason yoga was created.

Regardless of the style of yoga one practices, most yogis express feeling almost euphoric at the conclusion of a yoga practice due to its combined physical movement, breathing exercises, and meditative component. Remember that your physical and emotional needs are constantly shifting. Therefore, it is important to allow your yoga practice to transform and grow with you on a daily basis. Whatever it is that gets you to the space of honoring what is happening in your body and mind without judgment is the right style of yoga for you.

A Final Thought

Mindfulness, yoga and meditation are widely practiced around the world due to their contributions to our physical, mental, and spiritual well-being. These practices have become recognized by professionals in the medical, mental health, educational, and spiritual fields for these profound benefits.

Anyone can participate in these practices regardless of age, religion, race, ability, or socioeconomic status. All three can be modified to meet the mental and physical needs of anyone who wishes to enjoy their benefits. While it is incredible to visit a yoga studio or take a formal meditation class, it is unnecessary to travel anywhere special to participate in these ageless practices. Once one has obtained basic knowledge of these traditions, they can be practiced for free in the comfort of your own home.

It is important to note that Mindfulness, meditation, and yoga are not affiliated with any worldly religion. In fact, the disciplines of these practices have existed much longer than any documented religion in our world today. Over time there has been a mutual borrowing of philosophies and practices between Mindfulness and some religious doctrines, which allows one to draw connections between the two.

Despite commonalities, none of the three are directly related to any specific religious belief; hence there is no need for anyone to abandon their personal religion in order to participate in any form of Mindfulness. Transversely, there is no need for those who engage in Mindfulness to adopt or incorporate any new spiritual observances into their lives.

Mindfulness, meditation, and yoga are so universal that they can enhance any personal spiritual connection or interpretation of a higher power. However, these practices do not need to have a spiritual or religious connotation whatsoever unless the practitioner wishes them to.

Ultimately, Mindfulness, meditation, and yoga are deeply personal reflective practices that have the ability to transform our lives from the inside out. When we embrace them, these practices give us the opportunity to become more present to all life has to offer—joy, delight, discomfort, pain, and the beauty of everything in between.

It's a Practice

You might be wondering why the word *Practice* appears so much when discussing Mindfulness, meditation, and yoga. This is because regardless of how skilled one is at any, or all, of these activities, their teachings are infinite, and our dedication to them is a life-long process.

We never "perfect" meditation or any pose in yoga. Rather, we greet these activities each day from our ever-changing physical, mental, and emotional state. The goal is never to master these skills, but to look at what it is they can teach us in each moment. Our ability to learn from them never ends, and so we always practice.

These practices do not make perfect, they keep us present.

Mindfulness and
The Brain

The mind is a wonderful place. It is in charge of our thinking, decision-making, reasoning, and much, much more. Our minds work to keep us safe at a fundamental level when they remind us not to put our hands on hot surfaces. They also allow us to mentally stretch and sift through more hypothetical and abstract information that help us to learn and grow as intellectual beings.

When we contemplate all that the mind allows us to do, we notice that our minds are capable of far more than we give them credit for. Science agrees that our minds are the birthplace of not only our intellect, but also our habits and our self-esteem.

While it is important to understand what Mindfulness is, it is equally essential to fully comprehend why Mindfulness has such a positive impact on how we think, feel, and interact with the world around us. This section dives into the scientific study of Mindfulness and why it impacts us so fundamentally on a biological, emotional, and intellectual level.

The Mind on Mindfulness

The influence our cognitive thinking has on our overall well-being is often overlooked. Our thoughts have the ability to make us feel happy or sad; calm or angry; safe or at-risk. Our thoughts influence our emotional and mental health and can even affect our physical well-being. Thus, Mindfulness, which explores and shapes our thought patterns, can profoundly influence who we are as individuals. This, in turn, impacts our beliefs, our habits, and our relationship with the outer world. [15]

Despite the mind's constant activity, or maybe because of it, most of us remain unaware of the majority of our thoughts on a daily basis and the impact they have on our mood, behavior, and overall well-being. Increasing awareness of our thoughts is essential, however, if we want to support positive change to our mental, emotional, and even physical health.

Science has shown that the average person has between 50,000-80,000 thoughts every day. These thoughts begin the minute we wake up and continue until we fall asleep. Sometimes our thoughts even persist throughout the night and prevent us from falling into a deep state of sleep.

Of the 50,000-80,000 thoughts we have in our heads each day, it is estimated that roughly 80% of those thoughts are negative. [16] Even more alarming is that the majority of those negative thoughts tend to be about ourselves. Whether those negative thoughts are about the self, others, or events, it can likely be agreed upon that consistently thinking in this manner is surely not helpful in living our happiest lives.

Thankfully, Mindfulness gives us the opportunity to reverse this trend by increasing awareness of our thought patterns. This empowers us to think with more optimism and kindness. Due to all that science has learned about the human brain, we know that when we do something frequently, it starts to become an ingrained cognitive habit. This is supported by the study of neuroplasticity.

Neuroplasticity states that the brain is constantly being shaped by our thoughts and experiences. Every time we think, feel, or experience something new, we create what is called a neural connection in the mind. These neural connections are reinforced each time we visit them and weakened when we do not.

This means that the more we visit thoughts of worry or pessimism, the stronger these neural connections become and the better we become at worrying. Conversely, the more we focus on thoughts of happiness and well-being, the stronger these connections become and the happier we become. Any thoughts that we visit less frequently or ignore altogether will eventually weaken or disappear. This is why Mindfulness, being more aware of our thoughts, can be so powerful and effective.

Ninety percent of the thoughts we have each day are similar to our thoughts from the day before and the day before that. In this way, our thoughts become recycled and without knowing it, we establish patterns of thought that linger over months and even years. Mindfulness can help us break any patterns of thought or behavior that are not serving us well.

It is our thoughts that drive our habits, and it is our habits that eventually form our character and personality. Therefore, taking control over our minds to direct our thoughts in a positive manner allows us to shape who we want to be as individuals and members of society. Applying Mindfulness to the concept of neuroplasticity reminds us that we can actually flex and strengthen the positive muscles of the mind the same way we would train and strengthen the muscles of the body.

Just like starting a new exercise regime, training the mind takes time, and it can be uncomfortable to break old habits. With time and dedication, though, we can strengthen our capacity for positive thinking by repeatedly paying attention to our thoughts and channeling them in the direction we want them to go.

The Mind Mountain

To better understand the neural pathways of the brain, it can be beneficial to picture the brain as a mountain. A mountain is powerful and majestic, and there are numerous paths one could take to climb from the base to the peak.

The thoughts you have in your mind are like snow that collects at the top of the mountain during winter. When the sun and warm weather start to thaw the snow, the ensuing water gathers in streams and travels down the sides of the mountain.

When water moves in a downward direction, it looks for the path of least resistance. The easiest route is most often a well-worn route that previous streams of water have flowed before. After all, it would take much more effort for the water to erode a brand-new path through the rocky mountainside.

Your thoughts work the same way. Whenever you encounter an experience in life, your mind begins searching for an event from your past to use as a guideline for how to react. In other words, it looks for a neural pathway in the brain that has already been formed. This is why we so often repeat our past behaviors.

Mindfulness helps us forge new pathways in the brain and deliberately strengthen neural connections that are already serving us well. In this way, Mindfulness allows us to choose our behaviors through mastering how we think.

Understanding the Brain

Mindfulness has the ability to positively impact our behaviors and our mindset primarily because of its strong influence over our brains. In order to best understand how Mindfulness works, it helps to have a very basic understanding of the human brain, including its parts, its functions, and its development over time. [17] [18]

This section explores three evolutionary portions of the brain: the old brain, the limbic system, and the neocortex. Since the brain is so incredibly complex, this section does not provide a comprehensive view of this incredible organ in its entirety, but rather provides appropriate information only as it pertains to Mindfulness.

To understand the brain and why it operates as it does, it is helpful to look at the evolution of the human brain alongside those of other animals. This, combined with a basic understanding of human evolution, can provide important insight as to why humans are able to talk, process emotions, and conceptualize, while other animals are not.

Essentially, as animals and humans evolved over time, so did their brains. While different species of animals have different sized brains with different capabilities for reasoning and problem-solving, it can be agreed upon—with little scientific expertise needed—that humans have far exceeded other species in their brain development. The changes and growth that have taken place over time in the human brain have given people today more advanced thinking abilities than even our earlier human counterparts had.

Despite human thinking and reasoning existing in us at a much higher level than other animals or our caveman ancestors, it is important to note that some parts of our brains still operate at a very basic or primordial level—primarily those parts of the brain connected to our primitive need for survival. These sections of the brain react very instinctively and oftentimes influence our thinking without our awareness.

The part of the brain linked with our survival is often called the old brain. We call it this because it was the first part of the brain to develop in humans and animals. Others appropriately refer to the old brain as the "reptilian" or "lizard" brain because reptile brains never evolved past acting on basic survival instincts.

As long as animals and humans have existed, the old brain has been in place to ensure the continuation of the species. Our old brain helps us survive by providing us with instinctual knowledge as to how to meet our basic needs of food, water, and rest. This portion of the brain also activates the most basic biological functions our bodies need to survive, such as keeping our hearts beating and our breath flowing.

The old brain is hard-wired for survival and designed to protect us from danger. This includes alerting us to avoid or flee from life-threatening situations and provides adrenaline to help us fight and protect what is ours. In order to maintain our security, the old brain also encourages us to seek approval from important members of our community who may be tied to our well-being.

For animals like insects and reptiles, cognitive development stopped with the old brain. For humans and other mammals such as dolphins, elephants, and chimpanzees, however, the old brain evolved to also include more sophisticated functions of the limbic system.

Simply put, the limbic brain is the ruler of our more basic emotions, such as happiness, anger, and sorrow. It is also responsible for holding our memories, as well as regulating our body temperature and our circadian body rhythms. The limbic system is also where we house feelings of fear.

At the center of our limbic brain lies the amygdala, which is responsible for our body's lifesaving "fight-flight-or-freeze" response. When our amygdala is triggered, the sympathetic nervous system is activated, and our bodies have the immediate physiological response of heavy breathing and tense muscles. Our brains send a flood of stress hormones into our bodies, shutting down all of our bodily functions except those which are essential for immediate escape or aggression. In short, we get ready to either run for our lives, or fight to the death.

The amygdala is designed to act quickly to help us immediately escape serious injury or danger. The amygdala is triggered by any *perceived* threat in our environment and does not pause to assess whether a threat is imaginary or real. It allows us to act on instinct before even being consciously aware that danger is near. This is because our brains were designed to take in information and allow for survival without the need of thought or reasoning.

Having the ability to react without thinking is essential for survival in a life-threatening scenario, but this part of the brain has a hard time differentiating between a perceived threat and actual peril. This means that we sometimes react in fear without a threat actually being present. When this happens, we have to utilize the next section of the brain—the neocortex—to process through these fears.

The neocortex is the most powerful and newest part of our brain. It is connected to the old brain through the limbic system.

The neocortex contains our two large cerebral hemispheres; the left brain and the right brain. Together, these hemispheres play an integral role in our abilities to produce language, organize our thoughts, think abstractly, create, and use conscious memory. It is the last portion of the brain to fully develop and does not mature until early adulthood. Unlike the old part of the brain which works through automatic response, the new brain is responsible for the thoughts and actions we consciously choose.

The new brain processes the emotions we feel in the limbic brain, allowing us to respond to intense feelings rather than just react to them. The more advanced thinking capabilities of the neocortex gives us insight to help us better understand the complex interactions of the world around us, and thus allow us to experience emotional responses such as empathy. It is the neocortex that separates human beings from the rest of the animals on the planet.

Although some aspects of our brains are fully developed by early adulthood, the neocortex's fundamental capacity to learn and think in new ways never stops. This part of the brain is flexible and holds endless capacity for learning. In fact, the neocortex is able to shift, change, and grow with us throughout our lives. This means that regardless of our age, we always have the ability to learn new skills, and we greatly benefit from pursuing the opportunity to do so. [16]

The neocortex is also the part of the brain that allows us to practice Mindfulness. It is important to remember that practicing Mindfulness is a conscious choice and requires effort from most of us. When we integrate Mindfulness into our lives, new neural connections are formed in the neocortex which helps to positively shape our way of being.

If We Were to Design a Brain

If we were to design the human brain with the knowledge we now have about its different parts and how they function, it is likely we would restructure the brain to receive and process information much more efficiently.

As it is now, the lower portion of the brain—the old brain—receives input and information from the body and the external environment first. Since this is the part of the brain that houses basic emotions tied to our survival, it is very reactive. The front part of the neo-cortex, called the prefrontal cortex, houses our abilities to reason and problem-solve. Because of its location in the brain, it is the last to receive information.

Since information is first filtered through the old brain, we often feel emotional reactions in our bodies before we are able to process and reason through what it is we are experiencing. This is why we can "overreact" or quickly create a strong emotional bias that clouds our thinking.

If we could completely redesign the human brain, we would restructure it so that information went to the new brain, including the prefrontal cortex, first and the old brain last. This way, we could more objectively process the information with reason and perspective before tapping into an emotional response.

While we obviously do not have the ability to completely rewire the way in which our brains process information, we do have the capacity to positively impact our thinking with the use of Mindfulness.

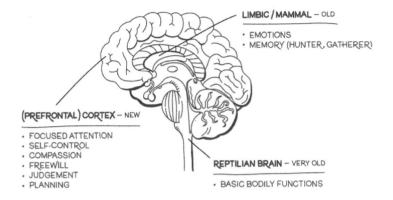

Mindfulness, Meditation, and The Brain

About sixty years ago, scientists began studying the effects of Mindfulness and meditation on the brain. Through their studies, they found conclusive evidence that these practices actually change the way we think through the brain's capacity for neuroplasticity. The connections that are formed during meditation lead to more positive responses in the brain when faced with stress and increase the ability to regulate ensuing emotions. While it was understood that Mindfulness and meditation led to these changes, it wasn't until recently that science revealed how this actually happens.

In 2013, a study was conducted by a trio of neuroscientists and psychologists from The University of Pittsburgh and The University of Carnegie Mellon. Their objective was to examine the relationship between Mindfulness and the gray matter of the amygdala. The researchers chose to focus their studies on the amygdala because previous research had found that abnormal or increased activity in the amygdala is linked to depression, anxiety, post-traumatic stress, and panic disorders. [19]

The study collected neuroimages of brain activity in over one hundred healthy adults who were given instruction in Dispositional Mindfulness, or informal Mindfulness practices applied to daily life. The brain scan images showed that after applying Mindfulness practices over time, individuals had less gray matter in the amygdala, meaning that it was less activated.

This is significant because as the stress response of the brain shrinks, it not only decreases negative thoughts and behaviors, it also allows for other areas of the neocortex to become more active—specifically the prefrontal cortex. The prefrontal cortex is associated with our higher cognitive functions such as decision-making and emotional response. More access to our prefrontal cortex allows us to think more clearly, manage strong emotions more effectively, and create healthier responses to stress.

Another study was done by Richard Davidson at the University of Wisconsin. He wanted to better understand the specific effect that regular meditation has on the brain. To do this, he looked at the brains of Tibetan monks who, over the course of their lives, had practiced meditation for over ten thousand hours. Using an EEG, he compared the brain waves of the Tibetan monks to those of college students who had never formally practiced meditation. [20]

The study specifically focused on gamma waves, which are associated with healthy mental activity. Gamma waves are the fastest waves produced in your brain, and they are activated when your brain is processing information.

Active gamma waves signal that you have reached "peak concentration" and mental focus. [21]

When the results of the EEG scans came in, the difference in brain waves between the two groups was significant. The monks' brains produced gamma waves at a rate thirty times higher than those of the college students. Furthermore, the rate of healthy brain waves in the monks was markedly higher than ever previously recorded in a person before.

Next, Davidson introduced the college students to meditation, then scanned their brains again. While their gamma waves were not yet at the level of the Tibetan monks, their rate was higher than before, showing that even small amounts of meditation can have a positive impact on the brain.

As seen in the studies above, consciously choosing to practice Mindfulness and meditation helps to change our lives by positively impacting the subconscious functions and communications of the brain. This can lead to a profound impact on our thought patterns, habits, and the nature of our character.

The benefits of Mindfulness on the brain are so widely acknowledged that many counselors integrate Mindfulness into their therapeutic sessions to help their clients work through challenging moments.

"Mindfulness allows me to be centered, focused, and calm with my clients. One of the things I love best about being a therapist is that I never know what the day will hold. Consequently, Mindfulness is an important part of my life because it allows me to adjust to whatever is thrown my way so that I can hold space for all of my clients.

"Mindfulness helps me to remain calm in the chaos. It also is a tool I teach to my clients so that they can learn to slow down, feel their bodies, identify their emotions, and create a safe space for themselves to fully process their experiences.

"For me, meditation and Mindfulness go hand-in-hand. They directly regulate my nervous system, which then helps me offer my clients co-regulation. As humans, we are designed to attune to the energy of the people around us. When I am calm, my patients sense this and they begin to take on my calm as well. Thus, it's essential that I stay grounded and regulated so that my clients feel safe and open to learning new patterns of thinking and being.

"Mindfulness also gives us the gift of presence. In a world that's built for distraction and escape, Mindfulness gives us the gift of attuning to the present and learning to live in the moment. Mindfulness helps us to slow down and identify what is happening the body and mind so that we can make a plan to move towards peace, healing, and growth."

-Laura Burton,
Therapist, Colorado

Peace of Mind

To further understand how meditation and Mindfulness benefit us, it is important to remember why our bodies experience stress. Quite simply, the brain automatically responds whenever there is a perceived threat in our environment. For animals in the wild, this is very helpful in escaping from predators. For cavemen, this also helped them to run away from danger and stopped them from walking too close to the edge of a cliff.

In the modern world there are fewer threats to our immediate survival than there were for our ancestors, but our fight-flight-or-freeze response is still activated whenever we sense danger. At its most helpful, this primal instinct tells us to swerve to avoid oncoming traffic. It also alerts us to double check that we have added the correct recipients before sending an important email. However, all too often fight-flight-or-freeze is triggered by mundane daily tasks when we imagine a threat to be present, especially if we become concerned about perceived criticism or fearful of a negative consequence.

The old brain is still primarily fear-based and is designed to keep us safe. However, the old brain is not designed to differentiate between a perceived threat and actual peril. If left unchecked, our tendency to fall into fight-flight-or-freeze mode can cause unnecessary physical strain on our bodies as well as creates chronic stress and anxiety in our psyches.

This brings us back to meditation and Mindfulness. From birth, our brains survey the world around us in order to identify potential threats. Neural connections are formed in the brain based on what we see and learn. Often these connections are very helpful. For example, we quickly learn that we will burn our hand if we touch a hot stove. Our brain remembers this important lesson so that we don't touch a hot stove in the future.

Other times, however, a life experience can lead us to create an unhelpful or untrue neural connection based on our perception. When this happens, we may have to unlearn what we once believed to be true.

For example, if your boss asks you to come to her office one day, and you are reprimanded for an error you made at work, your brain remembers and "learns" from this experience. Therefore, the next time your boss calls you to her office, your brain sends your body a stress response often manifesting as fight-flight-or freeze mode. Regardless of whether or not you receive critical feedback from your boss, it is quite possible that your brain has created a fear-based response for whenever your boss is near, and you instinctively begin to panic.

In this instance, an unhelpful neural connection has been formed and you experience stress whenever you are in the presence of your boss. The fear is irrational, yet it is real in your mind, and to support your growth emotionally, it must be unlearned. Meditation and Mindfulness can help you to do just that.

Meditation and Mindfulness teach your brain to pause and watch your thoughts when you are uncomfortable in a situation. This pause creates space for you to rationally assess why you are reacting in the manner which you are. It loosens the grip on the negative neural connection, allowing you to see the situation from a different perspective and assess new ways you could respond.

Once you pick a different response, your brain remembers this. The next time your boss approaches you, you will recognize she is not a threat, allowing your mind to recall your options rather than to immediately panic.

Furthermore, when you repeatedly choose a new way to think or behave, it becomes the new, healthier reaction your brain instinctively turns to in that situation.

While Mindfulness and meditation cannot eliminate all stress from your life, nor will it rid you of all negative reactions, it can help you to manage stress and empower you to respond more consciously to strong emotions. Mindfulness and meditation help to support positive thinking through stronger positive neural connections in the brain, which helps create a sunnier disposition to life. Mindfulness is a beautiful tool that can help you support a happier and healthier mental and physical lifestyle.

Mindful at Any Age

Regardless of our age, Mindfulness practices help us adapt to the constant changes that occur in our bodies, minds, brains, and emotions as we face new stressors and challenges in the world.

Some believe Mindfulness is the natural state into which we are born and that we slowly drift away from this mindset over time. From birth, babies constantly use their five senses to observe and learn from their physical environment. If you watch a child interact with the world, there is no question that they are fascinated by and enchanted with the present moment. A very young child does not worry about what will happen in the future, nor are they concerned about the past. They simply delight in observing their immediate surroundings.

What if we could keep this mindset throughout our whole lives? What if we could teach children to stay grounded in the present moment? What if we could teach teens to find physical and emotional stillness in the midst of turmoil? What if we could teach our adult minds to block out the frantic noises of society and recognize what is important in the here and now? We can—and the secret to this lies in Mindfulness.

Mindfulness for Children

As mentioned in the section, "Understanding the Brain," there are certain automatic functions of our physical bodies that happen without any thought or deliberate effort. Meaning that the brain, for the most part, automatically communicates with essential organs and systems within our body to operate and keep us alive. However, other essential skills, such as learning how to name our emotions and interact with others in society, must be learned.

While adults can intentionally decide to be calmer and more present in the moment, children do not yet have the skill set to do so independently. They must be given direct instruction and shown how to practice these skills. The implementation of things such as emotional regulation, gratitude, and compromise are skills we hopefully learn in childhood. No matter how you look at it, adult guidance is almost always critical for helping children to learn the social-emotional skills required for a lifetime of success.

Toddler yoga classes are a great way to introduce Mindfulness to children in their early years. Toddler yoga classes, which can take the form of a family yoga class or a parent-and-me session, provide a safe space to nurture a positive relationship between an adult and child. The physical component of yoga aids children as they develop their gross motor skills and provides the opportunity for young minds to engage in structured play time in order to practice important social skills.

Toddler yoga classes also offer meaningful Mindfulness strategies that can translate to life outside of a yoga practice. Teaching Mindfulness as early as the toddler years helps young children learn to identify what it looks like to be calm. By copying the actions of a mindful adult, toddlers can learn age-appropriate emotional regulation skills, such as taking a deep breath.

As children grow, they often inherit a hectic schedule—frequently transitioning from school, to sports, to homework, to family dinner, and finally to a bedtime routine. Being involved in competitive sports, engaging in academic rigor, having playdates, and spending time with families are all known to have positive impacts for children. Therefore, we often do not recognize the stress that comes along with such busy schedules. The rushed pace of our children's lives impacts their happiness, confidence, and pleasure in life—but usually not for the better.

Noting the fast-paced nature of children's lives today is not meant to be a criticism of parents. Everyone is doing the best they can to balance the demands of society with what they believe to be best for themselves and their families. Rather, this is an observation of how children's lifestyles have shifted as a natural reaction to what is available and expected in our fast-paced society. Ultimately, however, this means that children often spend very little quiet time simply being with themselves. When they are offered this time, they often choose to fill it with entertainment like television or cellphones that passively stimulate the mind and offer no true rest or restoration.

Offering Mindfulness to children teaches them early on how to sit still and be with themselves—an essential skill that is often lost in the hustle of our present-day world. Mindfulness practices like meditation, or Yoga Naps as we call them at Challenge to Change, offer time and space in the day for children to simply be present in the moment and pay attention to their thoughts and physical selves.

Guided Visualizations are a form of meditation that takes participants on a journey in their minds. These meditations can place children on top of a cloud, or they can take children on a magic carpet ride to their favorite place in the world. Through these practices, Mindfulness encourages children to engage in imaginative thought while also guiding their physical bodies into a state of relaxation and peace.

In addition, Mindfulness practices like yoga help children to develop spatial awareness, promote inner strength and resilience, and increase their muscular flexibility and physical strength. Teaching children healthy ways to move their bodies through yoga offers them a practice that can sustain all types of lifelong health.

Finally, Mindfulness practices can help children be less reactionary when faced with strong emotions. Children are born with a fully developed old brain, which feels and responds to intense emotions very quickly. Their brains do not begin to develop the skills of reflection, perspective-taking, and compromise until they are in their teens. Because of this, children often innately lash out or panic when confronted with fear, anger, or sadness.

Mindfulness, which emphasizes slowing down, pausing, and observing one's surroundings, gives children concrete ways to calm themselves when they are upset. This builds a solid foundation of emotional regulation that the brain can naturally build upon as children age.

If you are reading this book, it is likely you have experienced, or are beginning to experience, the benefits of Mindfulness for yourself. Imagine how different your life would be if you had learned the skills of Mindfulness at a young age.

Children are our future. If we can equip these future leaders with the skills to deeply know and love themselves, act with more compassion, and learn to focus on the present, everyone in our world will benefit.

"With my own two young children, as well as in my Pre-K classroom, I use the word Mindfulness regularly. We learn what it means in several ways including through practicing yoga. We learn about the importance of our breath and how it can help us to regulate our emotions and reactions. Mindfulness gives them power to recognize and accept their own mistakes as well as those of others and gives them room for forgiveness when mistakes are made."

-Holly Flood,
Pre-K Teacher and Yoga Instructor, Iowa

Mindfulness for Adolescents

Adolescence is a period of rapid physical, mental, and emotional change. Because of this dramatic growth, self-identity is a key concept for teens to explore. However, arriving at a healthy place of self-discovery during this transitional time is challenging because teens are actively straddling both childhood and adulthood.

When creating their independent sense of self, teens are deeply impacted by their peers. They are also easily influenced by what the media portrays as being attractive, successful, and desirable. Because they spend so much time looking outside of themselves, teens really need to be guided to understand what their own passions are. Mindfulness offers an opportunity for teens to look inward as they assert their place in the world.

Formal and informal Mindfulness practices can help teens pause in order to identify what is important to them. Something as simple as asking a teen to spend a few quiet minutes with themselves to define their vision of success is a practical Mindfulness practice that can deeply influence their future course of action and decisions. This helps teens to develop a sense of purpose and pride in where they are going in life.

Mindfulness can also help teens develop positive self-esteem and acceptance of themselves in the present moment. It is easy for teens to become self-conscious and critical of their rapidly changing bodies and appearance. Mindfulness practices such as using positive affirmations like, "I am healthy," or, "I am strong," can help teens appreciate their bodies. This can lead to body positivity or even body neutrality, in which one focuses on all that the body can do rather than what it looks like.

In addition to helping teens develop self-acceptance, Mindfulness also helps teens be more compassionate towards others. Metta Meditations, in which practitioners think good thoughts for themselves and others, help to increase empathy for other people. Teens are often criticized for being self-absorbed, so it can be very helpful for them to step outside of themselves and offer kindness to others. Pausing to be aware of individuals around them can also be an opportunity for teens to recognize that they are not alone in what they are thinking or experiencing in life.

Mindfulness helps teens to increase awareness of their thoughts, feelings, and emotions during a time when their bodies are experiencing extreme hormonal fluctuation. Emotional awareness offers the gift of emotional regulation—the ability to manage the way in which one experiences and expresses feelings. Showing teens how to calmly observe their thoughts, habits, and behaviors offers them a way to make more positive choices and create meaningful habits that will last throughout their lives.

Teaching emotional awareness is especially important for this age group because the portion of the brain that is responsible for decision-making and logic, the prefrontal cortex, is not fully developed until the mid-twenties. With strong connections to the emotional sections of the brain, it is usually easier for teens to identify what they are feeling rather than what they are thinking. Therefore, giving teens mindful tools to identify and express their feelings is especially helpful for these growing individuals.

This is important because it is estimated that of all individuals who experience mental illness, half identified having felt symptoms as early as age fourteen.[22] Mindfulness can be a great additive for other treatment options as it helps teens give voice to what they are feeling and provides tools for their brain health. Mindful exercises like "Affirming Who You Are," found on page 206, reminds teens that they are more than just their emotions.

Using Mindfulness to help teens explore the science of their brains and the more personal inner workings of their minds can help these developing adults understand why they might be experiencing strong feelings or behaving in certain ways. Being highly motivated by pleasure and short-term relief might explain why teens are vulnerable to boredom, procrastination, and often engage in risky behavior. Mindfulness gives them the opportunity to practice patience and learn the benefits of short-term discomfort for a long-term reward while creating a positive identity for themselves.

Teens experience a tremendous amount of physical, psychological, social, and emotional change in a short period of time. They are managing new social interactions, stressors, and life experiences on a daily basis. Furthermore, their bodies are developing at a rapid pace, which creates a challenge as teens seek to create positive identities for themselves. Mindfulness reminds teens to accept themselves as they are without comparison to others and helps them to be the best version of themselves.

"My first year of high school, I started practicing Mindfulness after hearing about the meditation app *Headspace*. I was fascinated with the idea of being able to connect with my body and mind, feeling rooted *exactly* where I was. I've always been a very anxious person, so being able to practice Mindfulness and have the ability to feel in control and at peace with myself became invaluable to me. After practicing Mindfulness for a few years now, my favorite mindful activities are journaling and silent meditation. Since my freshman year of college, I've consistently journaled every day. I find comfort in knowing I have a safe space that is just for me and my thoughts. Just ten minutes of self-reflection each day has become a way for me to check on myself and gain a lot of clarity about what I'm going through. Silent meditation, on the other hand, was something I struggled a lot with in high school. I couldn't stand the quiet. But now, practicing it in college, it has helped me feel comfortable in my own skin. Silent meditation helps to remind me that I am able and worthy to sit in my own thoughts with no distractions. No one tells you that when you get to college, you spend *a lot* of time by yourself. I thought that because of this, I needed to fill space with something every minute of the day whether it be through music, people, work, etc. Practicing Mindfulness helped me realize that by doing this, I was trying to run away from myself. Embracing the stillness has provided me with so much clarity about who I am and where I want to be and helped me accept that I don't have to do anything to be worthy of taking up space."

-Madison Kizer,
College Student, Iowa

Mindfulness for Adults

As society has evolved to present day, our lifestyles have increased in speed and complexity. With life moving at such a rapid pace, it is easy to get swept away in the rat race of to-do lists, achievements, and constant pressure to document success. Being immersed in such action-based demands can easily lead to disconnection from ourselves, our families, our inner child, and our core values. Mindfulness, however, can give us the tools to pause in the present and return to what is important to us.

Too often in life we find our motivation is not what interests or fulfills us, but rather our perception of what society views success to be. This includes being driven by pressure from family members or other individuals we look up to. In seeking to please others, whether it is society in general or a specific person, we forget what truly interests and ignites our passions. Eventually our internal light burns out.

There are several factors that can play into our falling out-of-sync with our core values and passions. Regardless of the origin of the disconnect between what the head tells us we should do and what the heart wants, when we lose sight of what authentically piques our interests, we allow our lives to be driven by our ego.

Motives driven by ego can be challenging to spot as they often wear socially accepted disguises. For example, wanting a promotion at your job because you have worked hard and want to continue to bring success to the company is different than wanting a promotion because you want to "beat" your co-worker and prove that you are the better employee. The external award of the promotion is the same, but the motivation is entirely different.

Being mindful of what motivates our actions can help us as adults to better align our external lives with our internal desires. Setting mindful goals makes the everyday tasks of our lives more joyful and meaningful rather than being tedious chores. Furthermore, recognizing the heart of why we are doing something can help us to put things in perspective, determine priorities, and save precious mental and physical energy.

Our time and energy are our most valuable commodities. If we spend these mindfully, we can build a life that feels authentic, safe, and complete. When we don't do this, we go through our daily lives with little awareness of routines and habits that are draining our energy. Mindfulness can help us pay attention to the small moments that make up our days, and then determine what is not serving us versus what is benefiting our well-being.

Mindfulness allows us to take inventory of the people, routines, and lifestyle choices that support our happiness and overall health. One way to do this is to pause and notice how you feel after engaging in any of your daily or weekly activities. Consider doing this after participating in a certain type of exercise, indulging in a specific food, or spending time with a friend or family member. Once you recognize the feelings tied to an activity or behavior, you are empowered to make changes and adjust in any way you need to keep your positive energy flowing.

In addition to creating beneficial habits, Mindfulness can also help us watch our thought patterns in order to make positive changes. As adults, our neural connections are strongly bonded and our ways of thinking, our habits, and our beliefs have become ingrained in our minds. Applying what we know about neuroplasticity reminds us that even though in many ways our brains are fully developed, the way we think can be changed and we are in full control of which direction it goes.

Let's put this into practice. Think of the first thought you had this morning upon waking. Have you had this thought before? We often forget that our thoughts are repetitive, but it is likely you have had this thought in the past. Moreover, if we don't deliberately choose what we want to do with that thought, it will probably appear again unbidden in the future. Mindfulness reminds us that we can deliberately choose our thoughts in order to think more positively. Positive thinking leads to stronger self-esteem, more empathy for ourselves and others, and a deeper capacity for compassion.

"Mindfulness is stopping to notice all that is around you without judgment—no "what ifs" or "if onlys." It just is what it is.

"This has helped me with my own personal acceptance of self. I have always struggled with my weight, and my frustration with not being what I considered to be my ideal weight affected my attitude. Now I accept wherever I am with my health and weight at any point in time because I understand it's a process. I take care of all parts of me and know that I'm a good person who is not defined by appearance.

"I also used to be overwhelmed because I thought I had to do everything. I was constantly multi-tasking trying to keep up with the image of who I thought I should be. I thought I liked doing things my way, and I didn't even know if it was okay to ask for help. Now, however, I have learned to let go of this chase for perfectionism and I am more mindful of allowing others to help me.

"My Mindfulness practice has also spilled over into the lives of my family. My son observes the world more because I do. I often find him by my side on our back deck watching the sun rise in the early morning, simply enjoying the stillness and peace. I helped bring this practice to his awareness, and now it's a part of who he is as well.

"My youngest daughter, who is often enraged by her brother, used to scream and rail at him and the world when she was upset. Now, however, I watch her go to her room and practice deep breathing to calm herself down because she's seen me do it and I've learned to prompt her how to do this.

"Mindfulness has truly helped me to step back in a really busy world—to take note of all the little things my children do and enjoy. I'm deeply grateful for all the time, space, and awareness that Mindfulness has brought into my life."

-Kristina Herr,
Elementary Educator and Yoga Instructor, Iowa

Finding Connection

Adults spend most of their day with thoughts constantly rushing through their minds. When we are consumed by thoughts (grocery lists, work, emails, schedules) we become disconnected from other parts of our body—including our emotions. This disconnect often causes us to be unaware of warning signals our body is giving us that we are approaching an emotional threshold. This is when we fly off the handle and overreact to small inconveniences that would otherwise go unnoticed, such as a person cutting us off while driving.

Using Mindfulness practices that increase the mind-body connection, such as yoga, can help us to notice the physical symptoms of strong emotions in our bodies. For example, tight shoulders or a clenched jaw might be a sign of stress, while a subtly upset stomach or a racing heart can signal anxiety. Through Mindfulness practices we can learn to identify the unique physical responses our bodies have to specific emotions.

When adults learn tools to manage their emotions, increase their personal awareness, and live life in the present moment, it is beneficial for all. Adults set the example for younger generations to follow; and adults in leadership positions teach all others through their example. Adults are also the emotional barometer for their families. When adults are in control of their thoughts and feelings, it creates a calm foundation for their families and others to rely on.

Benefits of Mindfulness

Practicing Mindfulness has been shown to have a profound impact on our overall quality of life. When we adopt a mindful lifestyle, it can positively transform the intrapersonal relationship we have with ourselves. This change can, in turn, influence our professional growth, the way we interact with our communities, and our personal lives at home. As you begin to implement Mindfulness into your life, take inventory of any positive changes you notice in yourself as well as those you teach Mindfulness to. Feel free to check them off below.

Emotional

Emotional well-being refers to an individual's ability to identify and manage emotions in order to live a well-balanced life. Emotional health is important as it directly correlates to the quality of our lives through its impact on our ability to experience joy, contentment, and internal peace.

Practicing Mindfulness can greatly help us to become aware of our emotions, regulate them, and offer ourselves grace in the midst of emotional turmoil. In fact, Mindfulness has been proven to increase feelings of well-being and decrease feelings of depression in both healthy and patient populations. [23]

Mindfulness can:

- Increase self-compassion
- Increase metacognitive awareness
- Decrease ruminating thoughts
- Increase overall feelings of happiness
- Provide stress reduction
- Decrease emotional reactivity

Physical

Practicing Mindfulness helps our bodies learn to regulate stress in a healthier way. Managing stress is proven to benefit not just our mental well-being, but our physical health too. By decreasing the amount of stress flooded throughout the body, Mindfulness is proven to benefit our physical health.[24] [25]

Mindfulness can:

- Boost the strength of the immune system
- Decrease the risk of heart disease
- Improve sleeping patterns
- Decrease susceptibility to auto-immune illnesses
- Reduce arthritic and other physical pain

Intellectual

As explored earlier, the brain is responsible for many of our daily functions. Mindfulness can help our minds to work much more efficiently as we move through everyday tasks. In fact, practicing Mindfulness can improve executive function in all people. Executive function is the set of mental skills responsible for focus, organization, memory recall, and planning. Executive function also allows us to smoothly switch focus from one task to another. [26]

Mindfulness can:

- Improve focus and attention (especially in those with ADHD)
- Boost working memory
- Increase the ability to learn and recall information
- Slow cognitive decline (especially in older populations)

Social

Social skills are used to interact with others. Having healthy social skills is important for our well-being and happiness as we benefit from connection with others. Learning healthy social skills at a young age is especially important as children explore their place within their communities. Practicing Mindfulness has been shown to have a positive impact on the ways in which we engage socially. [27]

Mindfulness can:

- Increase empathy
- Enhance satisfaction in relationships with others
- Improve respect for others and property
- Increase participation in group settings
- Decrease aggression and violence against others

Mindfulness impacts so much more than just the mind. It has the ability to positively transform our families, our communities, and our society. It is mind-blowing how something as simple as taking a few moments to pause, breathe, and notice our thoughts can create a radical difference in the ways we think, behave, and learn. Mindfulness holds many of the secrets to living a happier and more fulfilling life, and its wisdom needs to be shared with as many people as possible to help build a more peaceful world. There's no better time to start than right now.

Teaching Mindfulness
to Children

Introducing Mindfulness at an early developmental stage can have a profound effect on how children and adolescents live the rest of their lives. Reminding youth of the power they have to think more positively about themselves, the world, and others can potentially soften some of the growing pains many of us experienced as children, teens, and young adults.

Anyone, anywhere, who believes in the power of Mindfulness can share its wisdom with young minds. Therefore, Mindfulness can come into a child's life in a variety of ways. Parents can offer Mindfulness to their own children by making it a part of their family's daily routine or by attending Mindfulness courses and yoga classes. Some athletic coaches offer Mindfulness to their players to help with focus and sportsmanship during a game, and spiritual leaders can use elements of Mindfulness to assist their young followers in connecting with their higher power.

Contrary to what many believe, you do not need to have reached enlightenment or have the perfect soothing voice in order to share Mindfulness with others. In fact, you do not even need to be an expert on the topic! All that is required to teach Mindfulness is a willingness to engage in these practices yourself while keeping an open mind. Keeping an open mind means being receptive to the teachings of the practice for yourself *and* to the joys and frustrations that may arise when sharing these practices with others.

Whether you end up teaching Mindfulness to children in a school setting, at your home, or in a studio space, know that these practices will not always go according to plan. Therefore, we encourage you to offer yourself plenty of grace when faced with potential challenges and unpredictability.

Reflect on your own practice. Some days when you settle in for a period of meditation, your mind wanders, while other times it is clear. The same is true for children with their many thoughts and large emotions. Therefore, some days the lessons you lead will be serene and others might feel chaotic. No matter how a Mindfulness lesson goes, keep showing up for yourself and your Mindfulness students. Staying consistent in your teaching sends the message that you believe these activities are valuable and models the importance of practice and presence over perfection.

To help understand how Mindfulness can effectively be brought to children, this section explores how to offer Mindfulness to children in any setting, which includes teaching Mindfulness in schools.

"I started practicing Mindfulness when I worked as the crisis interventionist at a school. I used Mindfulness as a trauma-informed approach when working with my students. When I was struggling with my youngest son, I sought out individual Mindfulness lessons for him and began practicing more for myself, too. We both practice yoga and meditation on our own and together. Mindfulness has brought a sense of calm and peace to my boys and our family. It has taught our boys to show compassion and understanding for themselves and others. With Mindfulness, our boys are better able to calm their minds in moments of anger and frustration. It has been a beautiful gift for them and our family. We are eternally grateful."

-Ashley Leibold,
Educator, Iowa

Setting Yourself Up for Success

You are probably very excited about the journey ahead and want to dive right into teaching these practices. We say do it—but be sure to leap with intention by first setting yourself up for success. The following section holds suggestions to help you and the children in your life receive all that Mindfulness has to offer through the amazing lessons you teach.

Walk the Walk

Before teaching Mindfulness to others, it is very important that you first explore the practices on your own. This will allow you to *feel* the benefits of these activities for yourself and thus believe that they have value and purpose. It is important to find practices that resonate with you so you feel comfortable sharing them with others. In order to find Mindfulness practices that you enjoy, you can try different styles of yoga, participate in various forms of meditation, read books on the topic, or even explore Mindfulness-based apps on your phone.

It is also important for you to practice Mindfulness simply because it is a form of self-care. This not only models Mindfulness in action, it is a way to support yourself while you hold space for others. Remember that in times of emergency, flight attendants instruct passengers to first put on their own oxygen masks before assisting anyone else. This is so the passengers have what they need to stay healthy, which then allows them to help save others. Having a solid self-care routine in place benefits you and those around you. Self-care enables you to be your best self and gives you the strength to continue to teach through challenging or even discouraging lessons.

Moreover, practicing Mindfulness and self-care allows you to be authentic in your teaching. Children can tell when adults in their lives practice what they preach. They are much more inclined to try these practices themselves when they believe their teacher is doing them as well. Considerably the best way to share Mindfulness with children is to be an example of what it looks like to live mindfully.

It can also be meaningful to tell children age-appropriate stories about your celebrations and struggles with Mindfulness. Perhaps you mention that there are days when your mind wanders in meditation or share about a time you fell over in a yoga class. Opening up with your own stories allows the children in your life to see you as a human being—not just their parent, teacher, coach, aunt, or yoga instructor. You are a human being who is imperfectly practicing Mindfulness. Knowing that mistakes are a part of your process makes it easier for them to try Mindfulness too.

Establish a Routine

Regardless of the way in which you teach Mindfulness, consistency is key. Before you begin teaching, determine how and when these practices will take place. It is particularly helpful to establish a weekly or daily routine for your lessons as it will benefit both you and the children you are teaching.

When Mindfulness is a daily activity for children, they know to prepare for it in the same way they would for soccer practice or math class. An example of an effective Mindfulness routine is a classroom teacher who sets aside five minutes after recess for a Guided Mindfulness practice, or a choir director who begins every choral practice with deep breathing exercises. Allowing Mindfulness to become a normalized part of the day helps children to be comfortable with the practice, thus alleviating any resistance or anxiety they might feel if it was simply a one-time, and thus strange, occurrence.

Developing a consistent Mindfulness routine also helps to hold the adult accountable. It can be easy to forget or find excuses to not to do something when it is not built into the schedule—even something that is enjoyable and beneficial.

You are invited to weave Mindfulness into your routine in a way that feels authentic to who you are and how you interact with children. Perhaps you choose to begin each week with Mantra Monday, in which participants write positive affirmations and hang them where everyone can read them throughout the rest of the week. Or maybe you practice Mindfulness before each meal by encouraging those around you to first pause and share something for which they are grateful. If there are children in your life who struggle around bedtime, consider offering them a nightly meditation to help them fall asleep.

You can optimize your time and energy by aligning your daily schedule with your Mindfulness goals. Think logically about when your Mindfulness practices should occur and determine a reasonable amount of time for each activity. Remember, however, to be fluid and flexible as you go. Be prepared for lessons to take longer than anticipated or to go more quickly than planned. It is always helpful to have easy supplemental exercises readily available at these times.

Having your established routine will greatly benefit you and the children you teach. However, do not limit yourself to only teaching Mindfulness during this time. If you regularly offer Mindfulness in the morning, remember that you can still add a Mindfulness practice later in the day if inspired to do so. Staying open to spontaneous lessons that benefit your students in the moment can actually be Mindfulness in action at its best.

Explain the "Why"

Children and adults alike are more inclined to engage and commit to exercises in Mindfulness when they have an understanding of their importance and positive impact. For example, if someone believes they are only practicing yoga to get some physical movement, they will likely be inconsistent in their commitment to the practice. However, when they are able to see how the skills they learn on the mat positively influence their lives off the mat, they are more likely to dedicate time to the practice.

Find situational and age-appropriate ways to explain the benefits of Mindfulness to children. Tell Kindergarteners that breath practices will help them when they feel angry and want to calm down. Mention to teens that meditation can help improve attention and their ability to focus, especially during challenging times. Remind athletes that they can improve their physical ability through the practice of yoga and can improve their mental game through the use of positive affirmations. If you are working with a family, acknowledge that sibling dynamics can create tension and frustration within a family unit, but that Mindfulness can help individuals tune in to their bodies to recognize when they need to be alone and calm down.

The important thing is to find ways to relate to your audience. If you have learned some facts about Mindfulness and the brain, consider sharing this information with your Mindfulness students. However, there is no need to be an expert on the science of Mindfulness in order to effectively teach it or share its benefits. Offering the "why" of Mindfulness doesn't have to go any further than sharing how the practice benefits your own life. Any manner in which you can share the profound impact of Mindfulness helps others believe in and want to practice Mindfulness too.

Set Clear Expectations

An important part of setting your students and yourself up for success during Mindfulness lessons is providing clear expectations for the practice. The guidelines you set will largely depend upon the relationship you have with the children, the setting in which you are teaching, and the age group you are working with. For example, you will likely have different boundaries when you are working with your own children at home than when you are teaching a group of children in a yoga studio. Similarly, the expectations provided for a group of teens will differ from those given to preschoolers. Allow yourself to take all of these factors into account when creating guidelines for your students.

It is also important to keep in mind that Mindfulness is, at its heart, an exercise in compassion. Do your best to use positive language around the expectations you set. For example, try to avoid calling them "rules," as that has a negative connotation. Instead use words like "guidelines," "expectations," or "procedures" as they have a much more positive association.

When sharing your expectations with students, it is almost always beneficial to provide the reasoning behind them. This helps children of all ages to better understand what is being asked of them and why it is important for them to meet the expectation.

Consider the example of asking a class to stay silent during a lesson. You might explain that some participants struggle to focus during the activity when there is additional noise. Or your reasoning might be that Mindfulness is the only time that some children get to experience peace and quiet. Remind children that staying silent during the Mindfulness lesson helps their peers to concentrate or relax after the stress of a busy day.

When establishing expectations for your lessons, ask yourself what guidelines will help you to feel respected while you teach, what guidelines will help students to respect their own practice, and what guidelines will encourage respect between peers. If you are working with older children, consider allowing them to contribute to the expectations they would like to have for themselves and others during the lesson.

Some expectations, like using kind words, are very straight-forward while others are more complex. The expectation around participation is one that all Mindfulness teachers inevitably struggle with at one point or another. As Mindfulness practitioners, we know the many benefits that Mindfulness has to offer, and we want all children to engage in the activities to reap the rewards. Forcing children who are reluctant to participate, however, is probably not how to best support them in creating sustainable practices.

When creating your participation guidelines, keep in mind that Mindfulness is a vulnerable practice for many. Because of this, you might find that some children do not wish to participate in certain Mindfulness exercises. Our philosophy is to allow children to make the choice of whether or not they will join an activity as long as they can remain respectful to those participating in the lesson. We believe offering a choice empowers children to make decisions based upon what feels right for them and teaches them how to appropriately advocate for themselves.

Most children do make the choice to engage in most, if not all, of the Mindfulness activities. We ask the few that opt out to simply remain in the room and sit quietly during the lesson. We do not want to remove non-participating children or give them something else to focus on because we still want them to see, hear, and feel the essence of Mindfulness.

Often, non-participating students will join in on their own accord mid-way or near the end of the lesson. When they do, we welcome them in, no questions asked. Regardless of how or when a child chooses to participate, we strive to meet them wherever they are while continuing to engage the rest of the class in mindful learning.

Creating a Calm Environment

When trying to evoke a sense of calm for yourself and your Mindfulness participants, it is helpful to create a physical environment that embodies your intentions. Our mental and emotional energies are deeply influenced by our physical surroundings. Therefore, establishing a sense of calm in your physical space can help purposefully promote mental relaxation for your participants.

If you have ever visited a spa, it is likely that you noticed neutral wall colors with minimalistic decor, relaxing music, soft lighting, and perhaps even subtle and pleasant scents in the air. All of these physical elements are intentionally used to enhance the feelings of relaxation that guests seek to experience during their visit. For most people, it would be challenging to achieve a state of mental clarity and relaxation while sitting under bright fluorescent lights and listening to loud, intense music. While there is certainly a time and place for high energy, loud music, and bright lights, these concepts do not typically align with the goal of helping others to calm down in a Mindfulness practice.

While it is important to create a calm environment for your Mindfulness lessons, there is no need to completely overhaul your entire home, classroom, or office space into a zen-den for your sessions. We encourage you to simply work with what you have and use your creativity to design a special place for your Mindfulness practice and teachings. This space could be an entire room, a cozy nook or corner, or simply a decorated bookcase dedicated to storing your Mindfulness tools. An intentional space for Mindfulness, no matter how big or how small, is helpful in assisting the brain to transition from the bustle of daily life to the quiet clarity of a mindful practice. In fact, many people report feeling a bit lighter after simply walking through the doors of a favorite yoga studio as their mind recognizes they have entered a safe space intended for relaxation.

When establishing your space for your Mindfulness practice, do your best to create a feeling of safety and tranquility with whatever tools you have at your disposal. This could include doing something as simple as dimming the lights or playing soft music in the background. If you are able, consider investing in some items such as singing bowls, yoga mats, small bottles of essential oils, or individual meditation cushions that your participants can use during their practice. Integrating calming components into your Mindfulness routine will help shift the energy in the room and encourage a relaxed state of mind.

In addition to bringing items in for your Mindfulness practices, consider items you might want to eliminate during your sessions. Perhaps you allow Mindfulness to be "technology free" to give yourself and participants a break from our almost constant connection to screens. Asking participants to put their phones and laptops away while engaging in Mindfulness helps to eliminate distractions for the entire group.

While creating an inviting physical space is important, do not stop here. Be sure to also establish a safe emotional environment in which your Mindfulness practitioners can learn and grow. Mindfulness is an inherently vulnerable practice, and it is our job to make students feel as comfortable as possible. Just as soft music sends the message it is time to relax, gentle verbal reminders that this is a safe space helps participants lean into the practices.

Before offering any Mindfulness activities, remind your students that while they may feel uncomfortable at times, they are, in truth, very safe with you in this space. Reassure group members that you are here to support them in whatever comes up as a result of the practices. For most people, meditation is the most vulnerable of all Mindfulness practices. When sharing Guided Meditations, be sure to remind participants that they are safe at least three times throughout the reading. Knowing that they are in a protected space will help participants enjoy the practice and will encourage them to also engage in reflection.

Since Mindfulness is often an introspective journey, offering time for reflection is a wonderful opportunity for individuals to process anything that arose during the session. If you are offering Mindfulness in a group setting, consider using community conversation as a form of reflection. This is a great time for peers to share their thoughts and feelings in order to connect with others. This process of sharing and receiving vulnerable information helps to build trust and strengthens the bond between the group and yourself.

Remember that it will take time and patience to build meaningful relationships with your Mindfulness students. Before long, though, they will come to see you as a dependable and safe person whom they can open up to. To ensure the emotional safety of your participants, it is imperative that you have respectful boundaries in place for everyone in the group. We strongly encourage you to incorporate language that states bullying and teasing of any kind will not be tolerated. It is only with clear expectations of respect and kindness in place that you will be able to have open, honest, and authentic conversations with your students.

As with all components of Mindfulness, explore what feels right for you when creating your physical and emotional space. There is no need to adopt anyone else's interior design style or expectations for a practice. Be authentic in creating a physical space that will allow you to lovingly share your Mindfulness practices with others.

Tips for Teaching Mindfulness Practices

1. Know Your Audience: Remember that Mindfulness is not a one-size-fits-all practice. Keep your individual participants in mind as you explore potential lessons that will resonate with them. Choose themes and activities that are age-appropriate and of interest to your students. This helps to ensure that your students can identify with the concepts within the lesson in a meaningful way. Additionally, be sure to plan your lessons to match the attention span of your students; younger children need shorter lessons while older students can usually engage in lessons that last an hour or more. As you explore what works and does not work for your students, feel free to create your own lessons and adapt existing Mindfulness exercises to best fit your needs.

2. Let Yourself Be a Beginner: There are no "shoulds" for the best way to start teaching Mindfulness to others. The most important thing is to begin by offering Mindfulness in a way that feels comfortable to you. This might mean you find scripted lessons for guided meditations and simply read them aloud word for word to your students. Eventually, you may begin to veer off-script as you start to feel more confident in your teaching. However, you might not, and that is perfectly fine. If you are very physically active, you might find that teaching yoga poses to start might feel more natural to you. Just as with anything else in life, you will build your confidence and knowledge as you continue to teach. As you begin to teach Mindfulness, ask for help and use your resources—they are there to support you!

3. Use Vocabulary to Your Advantage: When teaching Mindfulness, it is important to restate and emphasize words that express your intended goal for the lesson. If you are teaching Tree Pose (page 215) during a lesson on balance, try repeatedly using the words "focused" and "calm" to help your participants embody these feelings. Using words such as "peaceful," "relaxed," "happy," "gentle," and "strong" throughout a practice helps your students intrinsically understand what it is you want them to feel. It is also helpful to use vocabulary that your students understand. For example, if you are describing a peaceful beach scene to a group of first graders, avoid using words like "serene" or "tranquil," as these are likely words that they do not yet know. Think about age-appropriate vocabulary to use as you design your lessons.

4. Take Your Time: Mindfulness, in essence, is about slowing down. When you first begin teaching Mindfulness, you might feel uncomfortable reading and speaking at a slower pace. Mindfulness, however, is not a race. Take *your* time leading practices so that the children can take *their* time in exploring them, too. Pausing to allow participants to connect with their breath and notice moments of silence are essential components of an effective Mindfulness practice. If you are not yet comfortable verbally pacing a mindful activity, consider playing a pre-recorded track from the Internet or a CD. As you build your confidence, you can record your own voice leading a lesson to play for your class. Using an audio-recording of yourself can also be a helpful assessment tool as you monitor your own pacing. Eventually you will be able to independently lead these activities for your class in your own voice in real time.

5. Calm Yourself First: Before you begin leading a Mindfulness class or activity, take a few deep breaths. It is challenging to instill a sense of calm in others if you are not first relaxed yourself. If you are able, consider taking a few moments to meditate before you begin leading others in Mindfulness. Taking time to calm yourself is a form of self-care, and it also shows your students that you practice what you preach. We live in the real world where issues pop up and emotions can be overwhelming. However, it is important that you calm yourself as much as possible before leading a Mindfulness class. For this purpose, commit to giving yourself a few moments to ground into your internal and external landscape before you begin teaching.

Mindfulness in Schools

For as long as schools have existed, they have been a place for much more than just academic learning. Schools provide a place for children to build social skills through interactions with teachers and peers. They also provide children with opportunities to explore new hobbies and interests and offer a safe space as children build their sense of identity. With all of the benefits that Mindfulness brings, it makes us wonder why more schools aren't teaching these skills in a place intended for learning and self-discovery.

Mindfulness is proven to positively impact children as they move throughout their school day. Teachers who use Mindfulness report that children come to the classroom more ready to learn because their minds are clear and calm. Academically, the students appear to be more relaxed and focused on the information at hand. Socially, they are more eager to engage with their peers.

In the last few decades, schools have realized there are factors other than mere intelligence that impact a child's ability to learn. Educators now recognize that true learning also depends upon a child's emotional and mental health. In order to support the entire student, Social Emotional Learning (SEL) opportunities are now integrated in schools.

The relationship between emotional health and academic achievement is so important that the educational system has developed social emotional standards that many schools are assessing in a manner similar to algebra grades. While the SEL scores do not impact a student's GPA, schools have deemed these skills important enough to a child's success that they are taught and documented throughout the school day.

Social Emotional Learning is the process through which children and adults obtain and apply the knowledge in the five areas of social competency. These competencies include self-awareness, self-management, social awareness, relationship skills, and decision making. While SEL and Mindfulness are two entirely different entities, the two greatly support one another as Mindfulness offers various ways for students and teachers to explore the skills of awareness, empathy, decision making, emotional regulation, and healthy interpersonal relationships.

In addition to benefiting our children in multiple ways, building time for Mindfulness into the school day helps to also take care of our educators. A lot falls on the shoulders of teachers because they are expected to do so much more than simply deliver curricular instruction. Educators also teach social skills, monitor student health, communicate with parents and caretakers, serve on committees, write and plan units of study, and nurture young hearts. This takes a tremendous amount of mental and emotional energy on behalf of teachers, and the toll all this takes on our educators significantly contributes to burnout within the profession.

Giving teachers time to practice Mindfulness, with or without their students, offers teachers the opportunity to restore their energy in a healthy way. It is important to remember that the impact of a teacher extends far beyond the four walls of the classroom. Teachers invest in students outside of academia—they cheer them on at sporting events, get to know who their friends are, and take the time to find out what makes each child tick. Burnt out teachers, however, do not have the mental energy to go this extra mile. Therefore, when we offer practices that support our school staff, we are indirectly supporting our students as well.

School administrators and personnel have one of the most rewarding and challenging jobs for the same reason—what they do each day matters. There is a tremendous amount of pressure placed on those in education today, and this can all too easily lead to stress and unhappiness. When this happens, it impacts the school culture, classroom environment, and student behavior. Offering Mindfulness for children and staff has the potential to transform school culture by providing not only room to grow and learn, but room to breathe, too.

We recognize the time constraints teachers face and the level of rigor and academic content schools are expected to maintain. Therefore, we hear, understand, and respect when schools express concern about how they can add one more thing to the curriculum, or take time out of the school day in order to teach lessons on Mindfulness. Knowing all of the academic, social, physical, and emotional benefits Mindfulness brings to children, however, we ask you: How can we afford not to?

We believe that investing just a few minutes each day in Mindfulness will foster more collaborative environments in schools, while also increasing individual academic achievement, student focus, and emotional stability for everyone. These are all important in their own right, but within a school environment they also contribute to fewer class disruptions and the need for behavioral interventions.

Consider this example: A student gets into a fight with a friend just before class starts. She enters her classroom, but while lessons and activities are taking place, her mind is focused on replaying the confrontation and on the anger she is feeling. Regardless of how interesting the lesson might be, she struggles to focus on academic instruction.

This inability to focus might even manifest as disruptive behaviors, which leads to more stress and negative thought patterns as she moves throughout her day. It may even be that this student wants to pay attention, but she does not possess the skills to manage her emotions and redirect her focus. Either way, she has now missed the important learning opportunities in the lesson.

If this student had been taught Mindfulness ahead of time, she would know some coping strategies to calm her strong thoughts and feelings so that she could focus. Additionally, if the teacher noticed the student's abnormal behavior, Mindfulness prompts could have been used to help her work through her feelings in a healthy way.

Mindfulness offers a momentary reset for both students and teachers. In this specific instance, exposure to Mindfulness could have helped the teacher and student connect so they could have worked through the situation.

Offering Mindfulness before there is an "issue", known as Proactive Mindfulness, helps set students up for success while they learn academics, build relationships with peers, and learn to process their emotions. In fact, people are less likely to retain information or learn a new skill when they are emotionally activated. Therefore, it is best to learn new Mindfulness practices when in a calm state so the mind can be open to learning. Once students have practiced a skill, they can call upon it as needed, such as in the middle of a heated moment.

Reactive Mindfulness, on the other hand, is designed to rein students back in when they have lost focus or control of their emotions. A reactive approach to Mindfulness is offered in place of behavioral intervention. Because of the success Mindfulness has in improving school culture, many schools are replacing detention with meditation. Additionally, in order to redirect student behavior, schools are also creating quiet spaces in classrooms with Mindfulness posters and resources, commonly known as "Peace Out Corners." Schools that are successful with these reactive strategies make sure to create a culture where these practices are not punishments. Instead, they are opportunities for self-exploration and growth.

Both proactive and reactive approaches to Mindfulness are beneficial to students. We see the most success, however, when they are taught in tandem. This ensures that all students have the opportunity to participate and encourages positive connections with the practices.

"In my fourth-grade classroom, Mindfulness is a priority, so I include it in our everyday routine. Sometimes it is for five minutes and sometimes it is for thirty minutes depending on what the students need that day. It is something the students look forward to each day. They can feel their bodies and minds become calm during this routine. It helps their mental health, their physical being, and they bring Mindfulness into their academic work. My favorite thing is watching every single one of my students let everything go and take deep breaths in our Yoga Nap, with no judgment toward each other and focusing on themselves and their breath."

-Paige Gallagher,
Educator, Iowa

A Note to Our Beloved Educators

We recognize that Mindfulness is not a magic pill that will automatically make every student able to manage their emotions effectively and be ready to learn. But it does help. We also recognize that teaching Mindfulness to a room full of children is often messy, disorganized, and loud. Be brave enough to embrace the chaos.

It is unlikely that a room full of first graders will sit cross-legged and breathe in perfect silence. You are going to have some wigglers and some who breathe like Darth Vader. Similarly, when faced with middle schoolers, you will likely deal with some sass and sarcasm. You might even have some outright refusal to engage at first, or forever. That's okay. As long as you believe in the practice and model what Mindfulness looks like amidst everyday life—including noise, wiggles, and push-back—you have done a fantastic job.

Just because Mindfulness doesn't create perfect classrooms or make a drastic impact every time, it does not mean we should shy away from teaching it in schools. Mindfulness is truly an important skill for students to learn about and practice every day. And remember, you are not alone—we have your back!

Mindfulness Activities to Support the Five Social-Emotional Learning (SEL) Competencies in the Classroom

1. **Self-Awareness: Label Your Emotions**

   Ask students to identify what emotion they are experiencing at the start of class, either orally or by writing it down. Utilize a chart displaying various moods/emotions to help younger children recognize and name their emotions. This exercise helps students to become more aware of their emotions and encourages them to check in with their feelings more often.

2. **Self-Management: Taking Five Deep Breaths**

   Plan a challenging assignment or task for your class to complete. Set a timer to go off every five minutes while they work. When the timer goes off, have the students pause and take five deep breaths, then have them continue with the task until the next timer goes off. At the completion of the activity, discuss with the class how the breaths impacted their work. Encourage students to continue to take these deep breaths as needed throughout their day. This activity teaches students a healthy self-regulation strategy to use in times of stress.

3. **Social Awareness: Identify What an Emotion Looks Like**

   Ask students to identify what it looks like to be stressed: Tense shoulders, wrinkled forehead, shallow breaths. Do the same for what it looks like to be happy: Smiling, laughing, loose muscles and joints. Continue the activity with other emotions such as pride, embarrassment, or anger. You can build onto this activity by looking at pictures in magazines or watching films on mute and working as a class to identify the emotions in the people you see. Talk about how you should interact with people when they are feeling certain emotions. This activity helps students to notice the emotions of others and learn to respond appropriately.

4. **Relationship Skills: "Just Like Me" Meditation**

Collect a variety of photos of multicultural students that are around the same age as the children you are working with. These pictures should show various races, religions, socioeconomic statuses, etc. As you display the photos, instruct the children to repeat the following phrases in their minds: "Just like me, this person has hobbies and interests. Just like me, this person struggles from time to time. Just like me, this person has dreams for their future. Just like me, this person is scared of something. Just like me, this person has people they love and people who love them. Just like me, this person is doing the best they can every day. Even though this person looks different from me, they are still just like me." This activity helps to build connection, empathy, and acceptance for others.

5. **Decision Making: No Right or Wrong Choices**

This activity helps students to reflect on the choices that they make in their daily lives. Place a small toy, prize, or classroom object inside paper bags—one item per bag. Put numbers on the front of each bag and staple them shut so that the students cannot see what is inside. Pass the bags around the room so students can shake each bag and/or feel what is inside. Then, place the bags at the front of the room. Systematically have each student choose one of the bags, then open to see their prize. Once all the bags have been opened, lead a discussion with the following questions:

- *How did you decide which bag to pick?*

- *What can you do if you don't like the choice you made?*

- *Was there a right or a wrong choice for this activity?*

- *Are there some choices in life that are right or wrong? What are they?*

- *Are there some choices in life that aren't right or wrong? What are they?*

- *When you make a decision in life and you don't like the outcome, what can you do?*

Teaching in Action

Sharing Mindfulness with others, especially children, is truly a gift. As a Mindfulness instructor, you have the opportunity to guide participants through much more than simply taking deep breaths—you are offering them important moments of self-exploration, self-regulation, and self-care. Keep this in the forefront of your mind as you explore these practices with the children in your life. Above all, know that you are making an impact on the youth of today.

When teaching Mindfulness to others, make sure that you have placed your own oxygen mask on first. It is often easy for "healers" and "helpers" to forget about themselves as they tend to others. As you begin to share Mindfulness practices, remember that you cannot offer your students that which you do not have yourself. Commit to filling your own emotional cup so that you can continue to share your kindness and passion with others.

When sharing these practices, embrace the imperfections and the messiness that arise. Laugh at yourself when you make a mistake while teaching a lesson, take deep breaths when things do not go according to plan, and, most importantly, continue to show up for yourself and your students. When you are able to do this, you are truly an example of what it means to live mindfully. By choosing to embrace a life of Mindfulness and sharing these practices with others, you are making an important difference in our world. You are a change-maker.

Teaching Children with ACES

Schools and society have recently become much more aware of the negative impact trauma has on the physical, social, cognitive, and emotional development of children. This realization has led to widespread recognition that extra care must be taken when interacting with children who have a history of Adverse Childhood Experiences (or ACEs).

In simplest terms, an Adverse Childhood Experience is any traumatic encounter that causes distress and leaves a child unable to control what is happening to him or herself. There are a wide variety of experiences that are considered ACEs. These experiences are typically identified as one of three main categories— abuse, neglect, and household dysfunction. Examples of ACEs include, but are not limited to, divorce, physical or emotional abuse and neglect, substance abuse, sexual abuse, incarceration of a family member, and the presence of mental illness in the home.

A child's ACE score is determined by the number of ways he or she has encountered neglect, abuse, or household dysfunction. Children who experience and live with trauma approach life and learning very differently. These children in particular might be resistant to engaging in Mindfulness practices, but they arguably need them the most. When you know you are working with a child who has a background of ACEs, there are several steps you can take to make the learning environment more comfortable for them.

Tips for Teaching Children With High Ace Scores

1. **Introduce Yourself:** Be extra personal when you meet the child for the first time, whether this is one-on-one or in a group setting.

2. **Be Overprepared:** Plan and practice your lessons so you can move through transitions quickly. Children with ACES often experience anxiety and struggle to focus during unstructured time. Allowing your lesson to move quickly will keep them engaged and help keep anxiety at bay.

3. **Tell Them What to Expect:** Children with ACEs do not like unexpected surprises or feeling a lack of control. In order to help these children feel safe, tell the class ahead of time what the schedule for the lesson is and what activities will be taking place. In addition, always give a warning before transitioning between tasks.

4. **Use Positive Reinforcement:** Acknowledge positive behaviors instead of drawing attention to negative behaviors as often as possible. Children with ACEs need to celebrate even the smallest accomplishment. Be as specific as possible when offering praise, and make sure to be sincere in your delivery.

5. **Meet Students Where They Are:** Remember that Mindfulness is a vulnerable practice and children with high ACE scores might not engage with the lessons in the same way as their peers. Offer them whatever empathy and compassion you can—especially when correcting any disruptive behaviors. These children are doing the best they can. Be patient with them as building trust takes time. Be patient with yourself in this process, too!

Mindfulness Practices

While the ultimate goal is to become so familiar and comfortable with Mindfulness that you are habitually integrating informal practices into your daily life, it is important to create space for formal practices on a regular basis as well. Here are formal practices that you can practice yourself or teach to others in your life to help instill a more mindful way of living.

Explore the five ways we formally teach Mindfulness at Challenge to Change:

1. Teaching Mindfulness Through Breath Practices

2. Teaching Mindfulness Through Movement

3. Teaching Mindfulness Through Sensory Experiences

4. Teaching Mindfulness with Yoga Naps

5. Teaching Mindfulness for Brain and Heart Power

A Reminder to Stay Open

While these practices offer great ways for you to share Mindfulness with children, remember that teaching is a reciprocal relationship; meaning that your students will also be teaching you. Children have a marvelous way of viewing and interacting with the world. Their curiosity and unique insights may profoundly impact the way you come to interpret Mindfulness. Learn to let go of your expectations for how lessons should go, and you might be amazed to see what naturally evolves. We encourage you to allow time for playful exploration, creativity, and laughter. Most importantly, be present with the children in your life as you walk the path of Mindfulness together.

Teaching Mindfulness Through Breath Practices

The physical body responds to mental and emotional stress in various ways. Stress can manifest itself as tight shoulders, a clenched jaw, sweaty palms, an increased heart rate, and shallow breathing. It is common for people to breathe shallowly in and out of their chests without realizing it, especially when stressed or worried. However, a much healthier and more effective form of breathing takes place when we breathe deeply into the lower abdominal region of our bodies.

Breathing in this manner is often referred to as belly breathing, diaphragmatic breathing, or abdominal breathing. During belly breathing, the abdomen naturally rises and falls with the inhales and exhales, mirroring waves on the ocean. Most of us do not breathe deeply into our bellies because we are attempting to maintain the image of a flat tummy. In this effort to hold ourselves in, we suck in our breath, which prevents us from reaping the benefits of deep breathing. Breathing deeply into the belly actually calms the body and the mind by activating the parasympathetic, or rest and restore, nervous system. [28]

Breathing is one of the simplest and most effective ways to practice Mindfulness, as it very quickly and effectively calms the nervous system. Deep abdominal breathing brings fresh oxygen to the body and mind. When it does, it sends a message to the body that it can relax. Mindful breathing can be as simple as paying attention to the natural flow of the breath on the inhale and exhale. Bringing attention to our breath improves focus and can help regulate strong emotions.

There are various breath practices you can do to channel your energy in specific ways: There are breath practices intended to calm, those that energize, and some that improve focus. Some breath practices even promote a combination of the three. It is important to choose your breath practice based on the desired outcome for your energy. This applies whether you are practicing Mindfulness solely for yourself or are sharing the practice with others. To help determine which type of breath practice will be most beneficial, notice the energy from where you are starting.

For example, if you had a hectic day of running from one activity to the next, you will likely benefit from a calming breath practice to help settle into your evening. Similarly, the day before summer break, it is unlikely that a group of second graders will need an energizing breath practice because their excitement is already high. Instead, they might benefit from a relaxing practice to help calm their energy before ending the school year. The breath you choose can help to create balance whether that is within yourself or within a group dynamic.

The way you inhale and exhale is important in a mindful breath practice and influences whether it will be calming, focusing, or energizing. Calming and focusing styles of breathwork typically recommend that you inhale and exhale through the nose. This is in contrast to energizing breath practices, which guide you to inhale through the nose and then exhale through the mouth.

It is never too early to start teaching breath practices to others. Challenge to Change teaches breath practices as early as the toddler years. Children are often told to "take a deep breath," but do not understand why, so it is important to educate children that taking deep breaths can help to calm them when they are excited or upset.

Providing children with the rationale behind taking a deep breath can help them learn to use these tools on their own.

Since breathing is automatic to the body, it often takes specific reminders to maintain focus on the inhales and exhales. For all breath practices, it is most beneficial for the teacher to pace the inhales and exhales for the students. It is important to remember that young children's lungs are not yet fully developed, therefore their inhales and exhales will be shorter. Consequently, the teacher should adapt the cues to breathe in and out accordingly.

For ages seven and up, consider using a silent mental count to inhale for one-two-three and exhale for three-two-one. As students become more familiar with these practices and are more comfortable taking deeper and longer breaths, the length of inhalation and exhalation can be increased. Offering students specific cues when guiding breath practices is helpful for both the practitioner and the teacher.

Anchor Breathing

Much like an anchor secures a ship at sea, Anchor Breathing is a grounding practice that calms the body and focuses the mind.

To teach Anchor Breathing, instruct your students to find a comfortable seated position, sitting with a tall spine. With elementary students, cues like, "Sit up nice and smart," resonate; while with older students, instructions to, "Sit up tall and proud," provide appropriate cues for a lifted spine and heart.

In Anchor Breathing, students use their body as an anchor in a way that feels best for them to sit and breathe for five to ten breaths. There are four different ways for students to find their anchor.

Anchor One: Place the hands on the knees. Notice the breath as it moves through the body.

Anchor Two: Place both hands on the belly. Feel the belly rise on the inhale and fall on the exhale.

Anchor Three: Rest one hand on the belly, and the other on the heart. Feel the rise and fall of the breath in the belly and the chest.

Anchor Four: Place one hand directly above the mouth while the other rests on the knee. Notice the cool breath move across the fingertips on the inhale and the warm air pass by on the exhale.

Begin by modeling each anchor choice and guiding your students through two practice breaths in each option. Be sure to cue your students to use deep belly breathing.

After modeling and practicing each anchor option, cue students to sit with a tall spine and the anchor that feels best to them. Have students close their eyes and take five to ten deep breaths.

Pinwheel Breath

Pinwheel Breath is a practice that links movement with breathing to create a mindful and energizing experience.

To practice Pinwheel Breath, instruct participants to find an open space in the room where they can freely move their arms up and out to the sides. Once each participant has found an appropriate space, cue group members to stand tall and proud in Mountain Pose (page 215).

Begin by inhaling and raising the arms forward to bring them up alongside the ears. Pause, and then lead the group in exhaling and reaching their arms behind their bodies to come to rest down by their sides. Repeat these same movements for several rounds of breath.

Next, guide participants to move their windmill in the opposite direction with their arms coming behind and up with each inhale, and forward and down with each exhale. Repeat for several rounds of breath.

You can offer a challenge by encouraging participants to try moving their arms in opposite directions as they breathe. As they inhale, they will rotate one arm forward and up and the other arm back and up to raise their arms by their ears. As they exhale, the arm that moved forward will move back and the arm that moved back will move forward to bring the arms back down by their sides. Much like patting your head and rubbing your belly simultaneously, rotating the arms in different directions is an effective way to connect the right and left hemispheres of the brain.

Counting Breaths

It is common for our minds to begin to wander and become unfocused when we attempt to sit in stillness for any period of time—including when we are engaged in a seated Mindfulness practice. Counting our breaths can be an effective way to give our mind something to focus on so that we can truly become immersed in deep breathing.

Begin by instructing participants to find a seated position where they are sitting up nice and tall. They may choose to sit with their eyes closed or to leave them open with a soft gaze fixed on the floor in front of them. Slowly guide the group through inhales and exhales to the count of three. Cue the inhale for 1-2-3, and then exhale for 3-2-1. Repeat this five to ten times.

When offering Counting Breaths with children ages ten and up, give them the opportunity to count a few of their own breaths silently. Be sure to always model slow intention breaths yourself to help the group keep their breathing at a calm and even pace.

Mantra Breathing

Mantra Breathing follows a similar pattern to Counting Breathing. However, it replaces the numbers with a mantra, or positive affirmation.

Cue your participants to inhale and exhale with a positive affirmation, such as, "I am calm." To do this, you will inhale to the slow count of three, "I... Am... Calm," and then exhale at that same pace, "I... Am... Calm." Repeat until a sense of calm has filled the room.

You may choose to offer the same affirmation for the duration of the breath practice, or you can choose to introduce other mantras as you continue to breathe. Other mantras that work well with this practice are, "I am safe," "I am strong," "I am patient," "I am brave," "I am beautiful," and "I am kind."

For younger children, we suggest that you choose one mantra for this practice in order to help keep their minds focused on a single message for the remainder of the day. With older children, you might choose the option of offering a different affirmation for each breath. Use any affirmations that you think might resonate with them.

It can be especially impactful to ask older children to complete a few cycles of breath with an affirmation that aligns most closely with how they are feeling that day or at that moment.

Breathing with Shapes

Teaching breathing practices with shapes is a creative and effective way for people of any age to connect with their breath. Utilizing shapes offers a tangible representation of the breath and lends itself strongly to visual and tactile learners.

Consider printing out the shapes and writing breath cues on them so individuals can trace along the shape as they engage in the breathing practice. Breathing with shapes helps to focus the mind and soothe the nervous system.

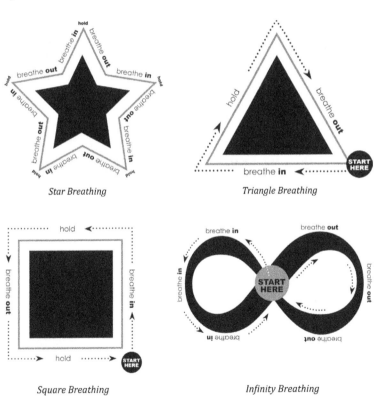

Star Breathing

Triangle Breathing

Square Breathing

Infinity Breathing

Mudras

Mudras are "Yoga For Your Fingers." We use mudras to give the physical body a meaningful task to engage with while the mind focuses on taking deep breaths.

Each mudra is connected to a different emotion or life skill. Therefore, we can use mudras to help look inside of ourselves and express what we are thinking or feeling at any moment in time.

When we offer mudras, we introduce three at a time. After teaching three different mudras, we ask each member of the group to choose the mudra that best expresses what is happening inside of themselves. In this way, mudras helps us to be more mindful of how we are feeling and give us a safe way to express and regulate our emotions.

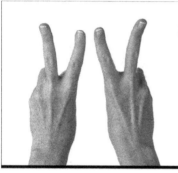

PLUG INTO
THE EARTH

PLUG INTO THE EARTH
Chakra: Root (Red)

WHEN TO USE
When you feel the need
to center your energy.

WHERE TO PLACE
Place your "peace fingers" into the floor or yoga mat beneath you. Actually "plug yourself into the earth."

WHAT TO SAY
"Plug into the earth is a great mudra to use when you are feeling the need to be grounded. When you have too much energy for your body to hold, and you have troubling focusing or sitting still. It is a really good idea to meditate in "plug into the earth" when you need to sit still and focus on a task or a test."

THE CHILD MIGHT BE FEELING
full of energy • overstimulated
in need of grounding

HEART CENTER

HEART CENTER
Chakra: Heart (Green)

WHEN TO USE
When you want to center
for intention.

WHERE TO PLACE
At your heart center.

WHAT TO SAY
"This mudra is wonderful to use
when you are setting your intention
for your practice. When you bring
your hands to your heart center
you are focusing on sending lots
of love and energy towards your
intention. You may use this if you
are feeling very full of love and
positive energy.**"**

THE CHILD MIGHT BE FEELING
calm • content • prayerful
meditative

LOTUS FLOWER

LOTUS FLOWER
Chakra: Throat (Blue)

WHEN TO USE
When you are feeling like you
are opening up your heart
to those around you.

WHERE TO PLACE
Base of throat, above heart center.

WHAT TO SAY
"The lotus flower grows from the
murkiest areas. It actually grows up
from the bottom of swamps! Even
through the lotus flower comes from
the darkest of areas, it is still able
to grow out of it and become a
beautiful flower that sits at the top
of the water. This would be a good
mudra to use if you feel like you are
coming out of a darker time and
now you are ready to shine your love
and light to those around you.**"**

THE CHILD MIGHT BE FEELING
open • ready to participate
coming out of a bad time

We always incorporate slow, deep breaths whenever we are working with mudras. Sometimes we also add some mindful movements to a mudra. The following practices are two in which we combine movement, breathing, and mudras to create a beautifully integrated Mindfulness experience.

Flower Breathing

Begin in Lotus Flower Mudra with your hands at your heart center and with all of your fingertips gently touching. As you inhale, allow your fingers to come apart, representing a flower opening its petals, and breathe deeply.

Imagine you are inhaling the delicious scent of the flower. As you exhale, allow your flower to close by bringing your fingers back together.

Guide participants through about three slow and mindful rounds of this breath. Again, remind them to align their movement with their entire breath to maintain a slow speed. Inhale to open the flower; exhale to close the flower.

You can deepen this experience by asking participants to close their eyes while they open and close their flowers. The true challenge lies in bringing all of the fingertips together simultaneously. This helps a great deal with focus and attention.

With younger children, consider lifting the open flower up to their noses on their inhales, and on their exhales closing their flowers and bringing them back down to their hearts.

Magnet Breathing

Begin by bringing your hands together in Heart Center Mudra. Keep your gaze fixed on a point straight out in front of you. As you inhale, move your hands shoulders width distance apart, stopping just before you can no longer see your hands in your peripheral vision. (With young children we refer to this as their "side eyes.") As you exhale, slowly bring the hands back together to Heart Center Mudra.

Ask participants to move mindfully. Make the connection between the hands and two magnets that are attracting and then repelling one another. Repeat this practice three to five times.

Invite students to try this breath practice with their eyes closed as they connect to their breath.

Teaching Mindfulness Through Movement

Mindful movement is any physical exercise that is practiced with awareness. Moving mindfully promotes a healthy relationship with one's physical body. Our bodies were made to move and to feel good while doing so; mindful movements remind us of these truths.

Mindful movement helps us connect to the present moment by activating our senses and aligning our actions with our breath. Moving mindfully can promote feelings of mental stability and emotional well-being. Bringing our attention to sensations in our body and the way it moves has many mental and emotional benefits: It calms the thinking mind, reduces overwhelming emotions, and is deeply centering. [29]

Teaching Mindfulness through movement is an amazing way to bring people of all ages into the present moment. Physical movement is an effective means to improving focus and concentration by burning off excess energy in the body. When individuals are feeling antsy or unable to sit still, going for a run or engaging in another form of physical exercise is often an effective way to rein in and redirect this energy.

Young children especially benefit from physical movement. In addition to burning off extra energy, physical movement promotes spatial awareness in their growing bodies. As children mature, mindful movement teaches children to appreciate and cultivate a healthy connection with their ever-changing physical selves.

In teens, mindful movements are equally as empowering as they are comforting because they offer teens an avenue to create positive relationships with their bodies. For most people, the adolescent years are filled with negative self-image and general disconnection from their physical selves. Mindful movements increase the mind-body connection, which greatly aids in promoting positive self-image, self-esteem, and overall compassion for the self.

No matter your age, movement is incredibly important for your physical and emotional well-being. Much of daily life in the modern world is spent sitting, and studies have shown that too much inactivity is detrimental to our overall health. Mindful movement practices offer physical activity in what otherwise might be a dormant day. [30]

Yoga is frequently used as a mindful movement activity. Yoga is different from any other workout because it relies heavily on the use of Mindfulness. Unlike stretching in front of the television or doing push-ups while chatting with a friend, yoga invites participants to focus on the breath, the physical sensations of the body, and identifying emotions that arise within the self as you move.

While yoga poses are traditionally practiced in a studio over the duration of an hour, this structure is not required in order to reap the benefits of mindful movement. Sometimes taking a mindful shape, or a single yoga pose, for three breaths is effective. For example, if you are feeling insecure, coming into Star Pose, which asks you to stand with your legs wide and arms by your ears in the shape of a star, reminds you that you are allowed to take up space in the world. Whether practiced as a single pose or as part of a sequence, yoga poses can increase awareness in the body and mind.

Teaching mindful movement to children can take the form of yoga, but it is not a requirement. There are various other ways to offer mindful movement practices, such as taking a mindful walk, doing a dynamic breath practice, or leading a team building exercise. Regardless of the type of mindful movement that is offered, be ready to adapt these practices to accommodate your physical space and the abilities of the individuals in your group.

Mindful Walk

A Mindful Walk can be added to any day! The best part about this activity is that it can happen anytime, anywhere, and without anyone else needing to know it is taking place. A Mindful Walk combines movement with sensory awareness in order to help individuals become mentally present, decrease anxiety, and develop a sense of appreciation for their immediate surroundings.

Walking is an activity we do on a daily basis. Because it is such a practiced skill, we don't usually need to concentrate very hard on our physical movements while walking from one place to the next.

Walking mindfully differs from everyday walking because it requires you to pay attention as you slowly put one foot in front of the other while carefully listening to and watching all that is happening around you.

Taking a Mindful Walk is quite simple; all you need to do is be silent, pay attention to what you hear, and walk at a calm pace. To lead this practice, model how to slowly walk while placing one foot in front of the other. Encourage participants to pay attention to the sounds around them, notice the temperature of the air, appreciate the different colors they see, and identify any smells they encounter while on their walk. Remind those involved that this is an individual activity, therefore they should avoid making eye contact with others and refrain from talking while engaging in the exercise

Feel free to offer more specific cues to help your participants enjoy the specific setting in which your Mindful Walk is taking place. For example, if there are other people in the environment, you might wish to offer specific guidance in observing body language and facial expressions. Or, if you are in a setting with an abundance of wildlife, you might suggest details they should look for within the natural environment.

Remember to let your participants know that it is okay if their minds wander while on the Mindful Walk. Offer strategies for these moments, such as pausing for a moment and then refocusing on the physical steps of walking.

These walks should be intentional and brief, and they can take place indoors or outside. When planning your Mindful Walk, consider setting a timer for two minutes or having the group walk the length of a hallway or classroom. The age of your participants will often determine the duration and location of this activity.

Yoga Sculpture

This is a cooperative group activity that can be used to effectively promote collaboration, connection, and compassion within groups of people.

There is no winner or loser in the Yoga Sculpture activity. Rather, Yoga Sculpture is a game that encourages collective creativity. The Yoga Sculpture forms a unique structure that is dependent upon how its participants come together in their yoga poses.

Find an open area, then ask for a volunteer to stand in the center of the space and move into his or her favorite yoga pose. Encourage participants to choose poses they can maintain comfortably for a substantial amount of time as they will be holding their yoga pose the entire time it takes to create the sculpture.

One by one, invite the other participants to join the activity by touching someone already in the sculpture and then embodying a yoga pose themselves. Encourage individuals to be creative in how they take shape and physically connect with someone who is already a part of the structure. For example, they may connect their foot to another participant's foot; or choose to touch hand to shoulder, elbow to knee, or even sit back-to-back.

Once the sculpture is complete, consider taking a photo of the final creation and encourage reflection of how each one of us is part of a greater whole.

Finding Your Center

Mindfulness exercises often combine movement with an intentional breathing practice to enhance the overall mind-body connection. This particular exercise, Finding Your Center, promotes individual body awareness and improved spatial perception.

To practice Finding Your Center, invite participants to find an upright seated position, either sitting in a chair or sitting cross-legged on the floor. Begin by offering specific breath cues to bring their awareness to the present moment. Consider utilizing the Counting Breath exercise, or ask individuals to place their hands on their stomachs in order to feel their breath move their bellies up and down on the inhales and exhales. Encourage participants to close their eyes for the duration of this exercise as it will enhance the overall experience.

On an inhale, guide the group to lean to the left as far as they can go without their hips coming off of the earth. On an exhale, slowly bring the group back to center. On the next inhale, guide the group to move their bodies to the right, and on their next exhale, allow them to return to center.

Repeat this process ten more times. Cue participants to decrease their lateral movement (how far they move side-to-side) as they progress through the practice.

Think of Three Things

This practice is designed to increase an individual's self-confidence by intentionally combining strength-building yoga poses with positive thoughts. A visual guide for the yoga poses referenced in this activity can be found at the back of the book on page 215.

Begin by guiding participants to take several deep breaths in and out of their noses while in an upright standing position. Offer the option of closing the eyes in order to better focus on the feel of the breath moving in and out of the body.

While continuing to focus on the breath, instruct participants to think of three things they love about themselves. These can be physical, emotional, or mental qualities they possess. Examples include, "I have beautiful hair," "I am a good listener," or "I am very artistic."

Transition the group into Warrior One. While holding the pose, prompt participants to remember the first positive thought they had about themselves. Give instructions to mentally repeat this thought in the mind several times. Pause for a few breaths. Move the group into Warrior One on the other side of the body while keeping their minds focused on this same positive thought. Pause once again for a few breaths.

Repeat this process with Warrior Two on both sides of the body, matching this pose with each individual's second positive thought about themselves.

Move the group into Reverse Warrior on both sides of the body, pairing this pose with each person's third positive thought.

Finally, allow individuals to flow through these poses on both sides of the body while reciting their positive thoughts in their minds.

Yoga Poses

Practicing yoga is a fantastic way to stretch and strengthen the body through movement. Similar to breath practices that calm, focus, or energize the body, yoga poses bring about a variety of physical, emotional, and mental benefits when practiced with intention.

Many people shy away from introducing yoga poses when teaching Mindfulness. This is often because they fear they might cause injury if they do not provide the correct anatomical cues to their participants.

While one does need to be careful about potential injuries when teaching yoga to adults, it is not as much of a concern with children because their bodies are still growing and therefore are very malleable.

To make things easier, however, the poses listed below offer scripted cures for you to read clearly and easily to your participants. Visual diagrams of these poses can be found at the back of the book on page 215. These poses have also been categorized by their intended outcomes: to energize, to calm, or to bring focus.

Energizing Poses

Energizing yoga poses are designed to wake up the mind and the physical body through vigorous movement and breath. A Sun Salutation is a series of such poses. This sequence of movement invites practitioners to open and expand their bodies on their inhales, and fold or release their bodies on their exhales.

Sun Salutations can be practiced as many times in a row as desired, but repeating the sequence three times will be enough to significantly shift a person's energy in a positive manner.

If practicing Sun Salutations with children, consider using the song, *Dance for the Sun*, by Kira Wiley. [31] It has an uplifting melody, and its lyrics move listeners through the proper steps of a Sun Salutation.

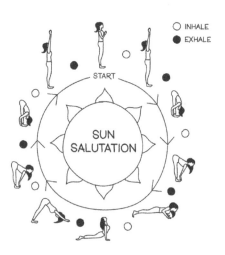

Sun Salutation Steps

1. Hands at your heart center.
2. Inhale, sweep your arms up to the sky.
3. Exhale, swan dive down into Forward Fold.
4. Hang in Forward Fold, shake your head yes and no.
5. Place your hands down and step, hop, jump or walk back to Plank.
6. Exhale lower down, belly to the ground.
7. Inhale; lift up to Cobra or Upward Dog.

8. Exhale to Downward Dog.

9. Walk your feet back and forth, breathe in the Downward Dog.

10. Bend your knees, take your gaze between your thumbs.

11. Step, hop, jump or walk into Forward Fold.

12. Let your head hang in Forward Fold.

13. Inhale and reverse your swan dive, reaching up high to the sky.

14. Exhale your hands to your heart center in Mountain Pose.

Calming Poses

When combined with deep breathing, these postures help to activate the parasympathetic nervous system, which invites the body to rest and relax. The poses can be practiced individually or as a series of poses together to aid in stress management.

Child's Pose

Come onto your hands and knees. Spread your knees wide and bring the big toes of your feet together to touch. Let your hips sink back so you are sitting on your heels. Extend your arms long out in front of you with your palms facing down on the ground.

Allow your forehead to come down so that your chest and forehead are resting on the earth. If you would like, you can walk your hands over to the left in order to get a nice stretch on the side of your body, and then walk your hands over to the right to stretch the other side.

Seated Forward Fold

Sit on the ground with a tall spine and your legs extended straight out in front of you. Flex your toes up toward the sky. If you notice that the muscles in your legs feel tight, you might choose to have a slight or a deep bend in your knees.

Pause for a moment to check that your belly button, chin, and crown of your head are all aligned. Inhale and reach your arms up over your head.

Pause and imagine that you are holding a large beach ball between your hands. Exhale and begin to fold forward. Imagine that you are reaching up and over your knees to place that beach ball on top of your feet. Allow your hands to then rest wherever they fall at the end of your exhale; whether that is on your thighs, shins, or feet.

Take several deep inhales and exhales, perhaps allowing yourself to fold deeper into the stretch as you breathe.

This pose only helps to relieve stress if you are not forcing your body to do anything. If you notice you are pulling yourself to get deeper into the stretch, see where in your body you can relax. Soften your neck and look down to enjoy the full benefits of this pose.

Butterfly Pose

Sit on the ground with a tall spine. Bend your knees to bring the soles of your feet together. Place your hands on the front of your shins, the tops of your feet, or place them on the ground behind you to assist you in sitting up taller. Pause here for a deep inhale and an exhale.

Feel your shoulders relax down your back. Soften the muscles of your face and allow your knees to fall further towards the earth if that feels comfortable and safe for your body. Don't force anything.

If this feels good, you can stay seated upright in your Butterfly Pose. Otherwise, you may choose to hinge from your hips and gently fold forward to bring the crown of your head towards your feet.

Remember that the goal of this pose is to help release tension, not create it. Do not worry about how far down your knees go, or how far forward you fold. Instead, focus on how much you can relax.

Focusing Poses

Postures in yoga that help improve our focus often incorporate balance. This is because poses requiring balance force us to bring our attention to the present moment in order to stay upright and stable.

When engaged in balancing poses, such as those that require us to stand on one leg, we are less likely to begin thinking about what is going to happen next in our day or use our mental energy to process an event from our past. If we did allow our minds to wander in these ways, we would likely fall over!

When practicing balancing and focusing yoga poses, it is beneficial to use a *focal point*. To find a focal point, locate something with your eyes in front of you that is not moving. Keeping our eyes focused on one still point encourages our minds to do the same thing.

Tree Pose is a common balancing pose that requires focus, strength, and stability. It can be practiced individually, with a partner, or within a large group.

Tree Pose

Begin by standing in Mountain Pose (feet pressed firmly against the floor, your head held high, and your hands at heart center.) Take some deep inhales and exhales through your nose and begin to relax the muscles in your face, especially in your jaw. In your mind, think to yourself the following phrases: "I am focused. I am strong. I am stable."

Slowly begin to shift your weight into your right leg and lift your left heel off of the ground. Open your left hip out to the side and create a kick stand by leaving your big toe on the ground and gently pressing your left foot against your right inner ankle.

You are welcome to stay here or bring the sole of the left foot to the inside of the right calf or the inside of the right thigh. Remember to keep your gaze focused on your focal point to help you stay balanced. You may then choose to grow the branches of your tree by extending your arms up over your head or keep them at heart center. Take a full deep breath in your Tree Pose.

Gently exit Tree Pose in reverse of the way you came in. Release your arms by your side, rotate your left knee back to center, and then slowly lower your foot down to the earth.

Find your Mountain Pose again, and then repeat on the other side. You might find that one side feels completely different from the other, and that's okay. Yoga is about finding your balance while also respecting the unique feelings of your body.

Tree Pose with a Partner

Stand side-by-side in Mountain Pose with a partner. Make sure both of you are facing the same direction with your hands at heart center. To begin, the partner on the left will balance on his or her right leg, and the partner on the right will begin by balancing on their left.

Once you have each found your Tree Pose and are balanced in your legs, both partners will reach their arms up to shoulder height with their palms facing out. See if you can bring your palms to touch while still keeping your balance. You might feel yourself sway as your partner sways, or maybe you will find that you help keep each other stable. Take three deep breaths in and out with your partner.

Once you have completed your three breaths, switch sides so that the partner on the left becomes the partner on the right. Repeat the same process so that both partners are balancing on the opposite leg than they began. If you want to test your balance together, see if you can leave your inner arms down by your sides and side stretch to touch the palms of the hands on the outer arms. Take three breaths with your partner and slowly lower your feet down.

Forest of Trees

Stand as a group in a large circle with participants spaced about a foot or so apart. Begin with everyone standing in Mountain Pose with their hands at heart center. When you are ready, cue each participant to move into Tree Pose while balancing on their right leg.

Once everyone is stable in their chosen variation of Tree Pose, have participants lift their arms up to shoulder height and touch palms with the people on either side of them. Guide the group to match their breathing with those around them and to notice how the balance of each individual affects the whole group. If one person sways, there is a ripple effect around the circle.

Perhaps remind the group, "We can use our circle of trees to help hold one another up. It's okay if any of us fall out—we always encourage each other to get back up and rejoin the group when we're ready."

Guide the group in taking three more breaths together, then switch legs to practice balancing both sides of the body.

Consider including a beach ball in this activity and asking students to pass the ball around the circle of trees without it falling to the ground.

Teaching Mindfulness Through Sensory Experiences

Intentionally activating the five senses is a powerful way to practice Mindfulness.

Sight, sound, taste, touch, and smell offer meaningful ways one can engage with the world. Sensory Mindfulness Experiences ask practitioners to use their senses in order to slow down and fully process each moment.

Sensory experiences bring practitioners to the present moment by awakening awareness in the body. How many times do you pause throughout your day to notice the sounds that fill the rooms around you? If you were to pause right now in this moment, what sounds might you hear? Would you have noticed these noises if you hadn't paused?

Mindfulness practices that incorporate the senses can bring about a variety of positive outcomes for anyone who engages in them. One of the most profound benefits of engaging in mindful sensory experiences, however, is that they can help increase our joy in daily life. For example, one can enjoy a snack at any time, but when one eats mindfully, the task becomes exquisitely pleasurable through heightened sensory awareness. The same is true if we take a walk outside. When we walk mindfully with awakened senses, we notice the pleasant smells around us, feel the gentle breeze on our skin, appreciate the warmth of the sun, and hear the quiet beating of our hearts.

While sensory experiences have the ability to enhance seemingly ordinary events, they can also help to alleviate discomfort in challenging situations. When we are experiencing fear or anxiety, it is most often because our minds are lost in thoughts about the past or the future. Using the senses to bring our awareness to the present moment can help us to calm down and regain control over our minds and bodies.

Noticing sounds and sensations in the environment is a great way for practitioners to evoke feelings of security and clarity. This can be especially helpful for people who have experienced traumatic events in the past.

Sensory experiences have the ability to soothe children and adults when they are in the fear zone. Activating the body's physical senses calms the brain to re-regulate and open the channels of more logical thinking. Rational thought brings our awareness to the present moment so we don't remain stuck in a repetitive cycle of replaying frightening scenarios from the past in our minds.

No matter the reason for engaging in them, sensory experiences can bring about pleasure through helping us to connect more deeply with our physical bodies. A weighted blanket is a great example of this. A weighted blanket is soothing because it creates the same gentle pressure and emotional release that a hug offers. Similarly, essential oils are commonly used in sensory mindfulness practices because they provide a pleasant aroma that lures us from our wandering thoughts to the here and now. Both of these are tools that tell the brain it can relax and become fully immersed in the present moment.

Opportunities to engage our senses are all around us. All participants need to do is turn their attention to them. Sensory mindfulness practices stimulate our senses and enrich our awareness. Through deliberate activation of the five senses, we are actually helping our senses to become more keen.

Sensory Countdown

A Sensory Countdown leads participants through a sequential process of activating the five senses in order to bring awareness to the present moment. This is a calming practice that can be used to soothe individuals during stressful situations, such as recovering from an anxiety or panic attack, or it can be used in daily life to enhance appreciation for one's current environment.

As you lead your group or an individual through a Sensory Countdown, you can have participants write down their observations, state them out loud, or simply make note of them in their minds. For individuals who are using this practice to alleviate stress or anxiety, it is usually best to have them respond orally or to just think their answers in their minds.

Instruct participant(s) to look for:

Five things they can see.

Examples: I see a pen on the floor, I see the lights, I see a picture on the wall.

Four things they can feel or touch.

Examples: I feel my shirt on my skin, I feel the temperature of the room, I feel my hair touching my face. I can touch this table, I can touch the wall, I can touch this stuffed animal.

Three things they can hear.

Examples: I hear my breath, I hear the clock ticking, I hear someone talking in the hallway.

Two things they can smell.

Examples: I smell the air freshener in the wall, I smell food from the cafeteria, I smell my lotion.

**If the participant cannot smell anything at this time, have them name two of their favorite smells.*

One thing they can taste or one thing they are grateful for.

Examples: I taste my toothpaste, I taste gum, I taste saltiness. Or I am grateful for my house.

Mindful Eating

Slowing down and bringing Mindfulness to a meal enhances the overall experience in numerous ways. When one eats mindfully, it increases enjoyment of the food and aids healthier digestion. Eating mindfully also improves one's psychological relationship with food, reducing your risk of developing an eating disorder in your lifetime. [1]

Mindful Eating asks us to slow down and carefully notice the sight, smell, texture, and taste of the food(s) we are consuming. It often initially feels awkward and uncomfortable to practice Mindful Eating because our society conditions us to consume our food and beverages quickly and carelessly.

Mindful Eating can be as simple as learning to eliminate common distractions such as television, work emails, and cell phones during a meal in order to pay closer attention to the dining experience. Mindful Eating is most effective, however, when practitioners focus on engaging all five senses while eating.

Any foods can be used in Mindful Eating. Popular foods often explored in this practice are raisins, chocolate chips, and mints. These food items are great for this exercise because they offer different textures from start to finish. Also, because these foods are so small, they are traditionally consumed mindlessly in handfuls. Learning to eat them in a different manner can provide quite a memorable experience.

Regardless of the food utilized for this exercise, consider following these guidelines: Before eating, pause for a moment and ask participants to think about where the food came from, who may have been involved in growing/making it, and how far it may have traveled in order to arrive in their hands. For example, a raisin was once a grape that is now dried—where was that grape grown? Who planted it, picked it, and packaged it?

Sound: You may choose to integrate sound into any portion of this exercise. For example, notice sounds present in the room when the exercise begins, recognize any sounds the texture of the food is able to create, or pay close attention to the sound of chewing the food.

Sight: With the food item in hand, use the sense of sight to notice the shape, size, and color of the food. Once participants have gathered information about the appearance of their food, ask them to close their eyes. This will help enhance their other senses. If they are not comfortable doing so, guide them to look at something non-stimulating, such as the ground or a blank wall, for the remainder of the exercise.

Smell: Without looking, ask participants to bring the food item underneath their noses and notice its smell. Its scent might be potent, subtle, or surprising.

Feel: Ask participants to take notice of the texture of their food. Consider asking them to roll it between their pointer finger and thumb. Is it smooth, rough, soft, or hard?

Taste: Ask participants to put the piece of food in their mouths but not to bite into it yet. This pause is Mindfulness in action. Instruct participants to notice the flavor of the food sitting on their tongue and to acknowledge their natural desire to bite it. They might also notice that they begin to salivate. Allow participants to take a single bite of the food and see if that changes the flavor it produces. Instruct them to take a second small bite, followed by a third, and then a fourth. After the fourth bite, participants may continue chewing and swallowing as they normally would.

Offer a moment of reflection for this practice. Ask participants if they found food to be more enjoyable when they ate it mindfully.

Mindful Eating can also be applied to the simple practice of drinking water. Notice the temperature of the water, ponder where the water came from, and savor the feeling of the water moving beyond the lips, into the mouth, and down the throat.

Close Your Eyes and Listen

Close Your Eyes and Listen uses attentive listening to pull practitioners out of their busy minds and into the present moment through the use of a resonant bell, singing bowl, or chimes. Using an instrument with a resonant sound is important for this exercise because it offers a mindful pause between the beginning and end of a sound, which helps practitioners learn to pause before reacting to an event when moving throughout the real world.

Instruct participants to sit up tall in a chair or while seated on the floor with their eyes closed or gaze fixed softly on the ground. It is important that your participants not be able to see any other members of the group during this exercise. Let them know that this activity is just for their own benefit, and they do not need to worry about what anyone else is doing.

To begin, lead a few rounds of slow mindful breathing, perhaps utilizing Counting Breaths to bring the group to the present moment. Direct participants to sit quietly with their eyes closed and listen for the sound of your bell, singing bowl, or chimes. There will be times when the sound is short or long. Sometimes it will be soft and sometimes it will be loud. Each time you play your instrument, invite participants to pay close attention to its sound and to raise their hands once they can't hear it anymore.

Do this as many times as you feel is beneficial for the group. You can also allow participants to take turns ringing the singing bowl or playing the resonant instrument of their choice.

Mind Jar

You may choose to use a snow globe or a similar object for this activity. In addition, you can create your own Mind Jar and invite children to do the same.

Begin by explaining that a Mind Jar represents the state of our mind throughout various emotional experiences. Sometimes we feel calm and still. When we feel this way, our mind is like the water in the jar when it is clear, and the contents are settled at the bottom. When we shake the jar vigorously, however, the glitter pieces frantically swirl around, bumping into one another as they move around in a frenzy. This is like our minds when we are feeling strong emotions like anger, fear, frustration, or extreme excitement.

Explain to children that they can use a Mind Jar to help them settle their thoughts and feelings when they are feeling those strong emotions. To use a Mind Jar, shake it to make the contents swirl together. Ask children to take deep breaths and observe the glitter slowly settling to the bottom of the jar. They may notice some pieces fall to the bottom quickly, while others remain suspended for a longer period of time. Although the children may have a natural urge to flip the jar over again before everything has settled to the bottom, encourage them to pause before doing so in order to let everything calm down before it is shaken up again. The goal of the Mind Jar is to give children something to focus their attention on while they breathe and allow their strong emotions to calm down.

To create your own Mind Jar:

Use a VOSS® water bottle. This type of water bottle has easy to peel labels, a flat top, and bottom that allows for the jar to stand on both ends. It is also made of plastic so it cannot shatter like a mason or other glass jar.

Instruct participants to drink the water in the VOSS® bottle halfway down the top of the first "S" on the label. This is a great opportunity to discuss the importance of water intake.

Fill the bottle with Vegetable Glycerin just below the top of the "S". This is the thickening agent for the jar.

Add a drop of dishwashing soap. This prevents the glitter and other jar contents from clumping together.

Instruct children to add glitter to their jars. Consider having them identify their emotions as colors. For example, "I am adding yellow because I am happy today and yellow is my happy color."

You may also choose to have special items, such as larger pieces of glitter, charms or beads, for them to add to their jars. These items can represent special people in their lives.

When children are finished, put the lid back on the VOSS® bottle and consider putting duct tape or washi tape around the top so children cannot open the jar.

Peel away the labels and enjoy!

Searching for Shades Scavenger Hunt

A mindful scavenger hunt is a fantastic way to combine movement with a sensory experience. A Searching for Shades Scavenger Hunt asks participants to use visual awareness to look for subtle differences in shades of a color. This requires keen awareness and attention to detail.

Collect a class set of paint swatches from your local hardware store. These swatches should all be different shades of the same color. Typically stores will offer one paint card displaying three to five shades or tones of a color. Give each participant their own paint swatch for this activity.

We suggest bringing participants into nature for this exercise and using green or brown swatches to color match. Give group members time to collect samples from the natural world that closely match each shade of green or brown on their paint cards. Remind group members that their samples should be small and taken with care to not disturb the natural environment. Once collected, offer time for students to share their matches, journal about the experience, or create a class display of their findings.

If done outside, use your surroundings to your advantage. You are not restricted to green or brown, but be sure that the color you choose is well represented within your scavenger hunt environment. You may find you are surprised at what colors exist in your natural environment.

Searching for Shades Scavenger Hunt can also take place indoors. However, participants will likely need to document their found objects by describing them in written form rather than collecting them as samples.

Teaching Mindfulness with Yoga Naps

Yoga Naps are a Mindfulness practice intended for restoration and peace. While the term Yoga Nap is a Challenge to Change moniker, the practice of settling in for a guided relaxation is widely used for stress management around the world. Unlike regular naps, the goal is not to fall asleep. Instead, the intention is simply to relax the mind and body through the practice of lying still. In adult studio yoga classes, this is often referred to as final relaxation or *Savasana*.

Many people have the misconception that the mind is perfectly clear and empty during a Yoga Nap, but this is not true. Our brains are designed to think, so we always have thoughts running through our minds. This practice teaches us to simply observe these thoughts without reacting to them. To do this, we present the mind with something specific, such as a song or scripted meditation, to focus on. These are effective ways to redirect our minds when our thoughts begin to wander.

While adults and older teens can sustain this practice in silence, studies have shown that, developmentally, young children cannot. They need something to which they can anchor their minds in order to practice calming their thoughts and quieting their bodies. [1]

Because of this, we teach children different ways to effectively practice a Yoga Nap. When the goal is to simply relax the body, we may choose to play a song, offer a progressive muscle relaxation, or provide a specific breath practice. When we want to encourage the use of the imagination, we read aloud a Guided Visualization that takes the children to a specific place and time through the use of the five senses. When we want to help build feelings of empathy and compassion, we rely on Metta Meditation, which is the practice of spreading love and kindness to ourselves, others, and the world.

No matter the focus of the Yoga Nap, at the end of the practice, the goal is for the participants to have had a time of physical and mental rest from which they emerge feeling calm and restored.

The positive impacts of these quiet moments are numerous for all ages. They can decrease stress, help alleviate anxiety, increase focus, nurture compassion for self and others, promote restful sleep, and improve overall well-being. [29]

The Yoga Nap is a Mindfulness practice that many teachers and parents have traditionally shied away from because they felt their children were not capable of lying still for a significant period of time. However, we have found that from toddler to adults, nearly everyone reports that this is their favorite part of practicing Mindfulness. For most, the chance to lie still with their breath is a welcome pause in an otherwise loud and busy world.

Our society moves at a hectic pace, and this is not always beneficial for our mental and physical health. Therefore, it is important to take time to set yourself and your children up for success in a Yoga Nap.

The following practices are scripted for your convenience. Read them as they are or adapt them so they feel authentic to you. Give children the option to stay seated or to lie down; to close their eyes or leave them open. This is a vulnerable practice, so it is important they choose what feels best for them.

Metta Meditation

Take a deep inhale through your nose....and exhale back out through your nose. Take another deep inhale through your nose, feeling the air move deep into your belly, and exhale back out through the nose.

Today we're going to practice Metta Mindfulness. Metta is the practice of spreading love and kindness. Spreading love and kindness is very important to do because it helps make the world a happier and more peaceful place. It's very important for us to practice Metta on ourselves, to those that we love, and to those that we don't like very much.

You can practice Metta anytime you want to. You can send Metta while you're waiting in line, when you're riding in the car, or even when you're sitting at your desk. All that you need in order to practice Metta is your smart mind and these four phrases:

May you be happy.

May you be healthy.

May you feel loved.

May you be safe.

It is always important to practice Metta on ourselves first, because it is only when we feel happy and loved that we can share those things with others. So, I want you to think about a picture of yourself. Maybe it's your school picture, maybe it's a picture you took with your family, or maybe it's a picture of you doing something silly.

Visualize that picture. Now I want you to say the four phrases to yourself as I say them out loud:

May I be happy.

May I be healthy.

May I feel loved.

May I be safe.

It's so important to practice Metta on ourselves before we practice it on others. When we feel loved ourselves, then we can practice Metta on others whom we love very much too.

Now think about someone that you love very much. Maybe it's your mom or your dad. Maybe it's one of your siblings or a special friend. Perhaps it's one of your pets. Visualize a picture of that person. As I say the words out loud, visualize that you are saying the phrases to that person:

May you be happy.

May you be healthy.

May you feel loved.

May you be safe.

It's so important to practice Metta on ourselves, as well as on those that we love.

Now here comes the hardest, but most important, part of Metta: To spread love and kindness to those that we don't like very much.

It's important to practice Metta on people that we don't like very much because often they don't feel loved, happy, healthy, or safe.

So, bring to mind someone you don't like very much. Maybe it's someone who has been unkind to you. Maybe it is someone who has hurt you, or maybe it is someone who you love very much but have difficulty getting along with. Visualize saying these four phrases to that person as I say them out loud:

May you be happy.

May you be healthy.

May you feel loved.

May you be safe.

When we practice Metta on someone who has been unkind to us, we often feel better, and we act with more love, and compassion, and kindness to those around us. Remember that you can practice Metta anytime that you want to. All you need to do is use the four phrases and see a picture in your mind of that person.

Now slowly begin to wiggle your fingers and toes, bringing awareness back to your physical body.

Tense and Release Muscle Relaxation

Make your body comfortable. Lie on your back with your legs stretched long and your hands at your sides. Take a deep breath in . . . and out. Close your eyes and allow your body to relax.

Today we are going to do a practice called a Tense and Release Muscle Relaxation to help our bodies feel as calm and relaxed as possible. I am going to guide you in how to use your breath, your muscles, and your positive thoughts to help relax your body from the tips of your toes all the way to the top of your head.

We'll begin with your feet. Curl your toes and squeeze the muscles in your feet as tightly as you can. Take a deep inhale while keeping your toes curled . . . then exhale and uncurl your toes to release. Let all the tension in your feet go as you take another deep inhale . . . and an exhale.

Now picture the lower parts of your legs—your calves and your shins—clearly in your mind. Imagine forcing your lower legs together as you tense the muscles there. Take a deep inhale as you continue to squeeze, and then exhale as you let all the tension go.

Do this for the muscles in your upper legs as well. Imagine forcing your legs together as you tense your legs above the knee. Squeeze tightly as you take a deep breath in . . . and then exhale as you let it go. Breathe and relax your body completely. Allow yourself to melt into the ground beneath you.

Now we are going to move on to your bottoms, or your "sit bones." Take a deep breath and squeeze all the muscles in your bottom together as tightly as you can. It might cause your body to lift off the ground a little. Squeeze tightly as you continue to breathe . . . and on your next exhale release. Feel all the muscles in your bottom relax as your body melts back into the ground beneath you.

Let's just focus on our breath for a moment here. Breathe in . . . and out. Inhale . . . and exhale.

Notice how your lower body feels. Does it feel more relaxed after having done this exercise? I hope so. If your eyes have opened during this activity, softly close them again. Let's move on to the rest of your body now, starting with your hands.

Continue to breathe and squeeze your hands tightly into fists. Squeeze all the muscles in your hands as tightly as you can. Inhale and squeeze . . . then exhale and release. Uncurl your fingers and return your hands to rest, palms up, on the floor.

Now stiffen the muscles in your arms as though you were trying to force them together. Squeeze the muscles in your arms, maybe even making your arms shake with the effort, and then release and relax your arms back to the ground. Let your arms go limp, like noodles, as you let all the tension go. Continue to take deep breaths in and out through your nose as you allow your body to relax.

We are going to move on to your shoulders and back now. Take a deep inhale and squeeze the backs of your shoulders together while keeping your shoulders away from your ears.

See if you can tense the muscles along your spine and into your lower back. Continue to squeeze and tense your shoulders and back as you breathe. Take a deep inhale . . . and as you exhale, let it all go.

Let your shoulders relax and feel your back melt into the floor. Enjoy how good it feels to just rest after holding on to that tension in your shoulders and your spine. Take deep breaths in and out as you continue to rest.

Finally, see if you can tense the back of your neck all the way up to the crown of your head. In your mind, visualize a golden rod of light stretching your head and neck long. Hold this stretch as you inhale, and as you exhale let it all go.

Your body is fully relaxed now. Your muscles are loose, and any tension you had been holding on to has melted away. Take a deep inhale . . . and exhale. Breathe in . . . and out.

You are at peace . . . calm and still. Feel your heartbeat slow even more with your deep breaths. Breathe in . . . and out. In . . . and out.

You can do this muscle relaxation exercise anytime you want to let go of any stress or worries you are holding in your body. You can do it lying in your bed, riding in the car, or sitting at your desk in school. Simply squeeze your muscle one at a time while you breathe . . . and then relax.

Begin to wiggle your fingers and toes, bringing movement back into your physical body. Rock your neck softly side to side, then reach your arms up over your head to make your body as long as you possibly can. Bend your knees and hug them tightly into your chest. Rock side to side, and then gently fall over onto your right. Bring yourself up to a seated position with your hands at heart center for our close of practice.

Floating on a Cloud

Begin to take deep inhales and exhales, in and out through your nose. As you breathe, start to feel your body relax, your mind unwind, and your heartbeat slow.

As you listen to my words, remember to take deep inhales in through your nose. Feel the air move deep into your belly, and then exhale back out through your nose. Do this three more times:

Inhale . . . Exhale.

Inhale . . . Exhale.

Inhale . . . Exhale.

As you continue to breathe deeply and slowly, feel your smart mind connect to your kind heart and calm your body.

With your smart mind, begin to imagine that you are floating on a cloud—a big, fluffy white cloud. Notice how comfortable the cloud feels as it lifts you high into the sky. Know that you are completely safe on your cloud. This cloud has been made especially for you and your safe adventure.

As the cloud takes you higher into the sky, visualize in your mind where you want the cloud to take you. You can go anywhere you want to go—just ask your cloud to take you there.

As the cloud carries you to your special place, you can tell it to go higher or lower. You can tell it to go slower or faster. This cloud is your special cloud; it was made especially for you.

As your cloud takes you to your special place, notice how you feel. What does this journey do to your kind heart? Do you feel calm? Excited? Happy? Peaceful?

This good feeling is always inside of you. You can feel it at any time, just by closing your eyes and connecting your smart mind to your kind heart and your calm body.

As your cloud comes to your special place, peek over the side of the cloud and look down on what is below.

What do you see? What do you hear? What do you feel?

Visualize all this clearly in your mind.

Now it is time for you to return from your special place. Ask your cloud to take you back. Remember that on your return home, you can ask your cloud to travel fast or slow; high or low. You are in control of your safe journey.

Ask your cloud to return you to where you are now. As your cloud slowly descends from the sky, take a deep breath in through your nose, and exhale it back out. Do this three more times:

Inhale . . . Exhale.

Inhale . . . Exhale.

Inhale . . . Exhale.

After your final exhale, stretch your arms up over your head and smile.

Boat Meditation
By Paula Purcell

Take a moment to find your most comfortable position. Lie down on the floor with your legs loose and long and your arms relaxed at your sides. Turn your palms toward the sky and open your heart to receiving this time of gentle peace.

Take a deep cleansing breath in . . . then slowly release and let it out. As you exhale, feel your entire body relax even further. Take another breath in . . . and let it out. Continue to breathe deeply at your own pace. Notice how your stomach expands with each inhale, and then slowly sinks towards the earth as you exhale.

As I count down from five to one, allow your body to grow heavy and calm.

Five . . . Notice the stillness in your hands and feet. Release any tension you have been holding on to.

Four . . . Allow your arms and legs to feel heavy and at rest.

Three . . . Relax your face, allowing any tension to fade away.

Two . . . Let your entire body grow heavy and sink towards the earth.

One . . .

Now imagine you are walking alone on a white, sandy beach that stretches as far as your eyes can see. Feel the powdery, warm sand beneath your feet as you walk towards the crystal blue sea. Hear the sound of the gentle waves as they break onto the shore and slide back out.

The heat of the afternoon sun kisses your skin and fills your whole body with warmth and comfort. You feel the delicate ocean breeze brush softly across your skin. The air smells clean and crisp, and you can taste the subtle salt of the sea on your lips.

A small, wooden canoe is waiting for you on the shoreline. As you approach the boat, you grab the paddle that has been left inside and slowly climb aboard. The canoe immediately feels safe; almost as if it were built just for you. You push the paddle into the sand, gently guiding the boat out to sea and towards the brilliant red sunset ahead of you.

The calm waves hug the boat, pulling it away from the sandy beach, leading you farther and farther out to sea. Feeling completely safe and content, you set your paddle down and slide off of the seat to lie down in the bottom of the boat where you can rest.

You close your eyes. You feel embraced and protected by the curved sides of the boat. The waves gently cradle you as if they were a mother rocking her newborn baby to sleep. Your body feels light, and you allow any stress to which you have been holding on to float away. You feel completely at peace.

After a short time, you wake and move back to your seat. You pick up the wooden paddle and dip it into the teal blue water, gently steering the boat back towards the shore. With a few deep strokes of the paddle and the push of a wave from behind, the vibration of the boat bottom gliding against the sandy shoreline lets you know you've arrived. You come to a slow stop back on the beach.

Now, as I count from one to five, slowly begin to bring your awareness back to the present moment.

One . . . Bring your attention to your breath. Take a deep inhale . . . and as you release, notice how relaxed and light you feel.

Two . . . Begin to bring movement back to your body by gently wiggling your fingers and toes.

Three . . . Stretch your arms overhead and take in another deep breath. As you exhale, wrap your arms around your knees and bring them into your chest.

Four . . . If it feels right, gently release and roll over onto your right side.

Five . . . In your own time, make your way back to an easy seated position for our close of practice.

Mantra Meditation

Lie on your back and relax your body. Straighten your legs and allow your feet to fall open naturally. Rest your arms at your side or on your belly. Feel your shoulders and spine melt into the earth. Softly close your eyes.

Remember to come to your breath. Begin to take deep inhales and exhales in and out through your nose. Feel your body continue to relax, your mind unwind, and your heartbeat slow as you focus on taking deep breaths in and out through your nose.

Breathe in through your nose . . . and out. Breathe in . . . and out.

Mantras are words you say over and over to yourself in order to help your thinking become more positive. Mantras begin with the words "I am", and the third word is what you want to become.

There are so many wonderful mantras that can help us think more positively about ourselves and the world around us. Today we are going to go through several of these mantras. After I say each mantra, please repeat it in your mind quietly or whisper it softly to yourself.

Are you ready?

I am safe.

I am grounded.

I am healthy.

I am strong.

I am enough.

I am courageous.

I am creative.

I am talented.

I am calm.

I am trying.

I am cooperative.

I am knowing.

I am friendly.

I am loving.

I am grateful.

I am joyful.

I am respectful.

I am kind.

I am honest.

I am positive.

I am smart.

I am responsible.

I am unique.

I am beautiful.

I am peaceful.

I am trustworthy.

I am powerful.

I am awesome.

Our brains are powerful and amazing, and we can make them even more powerful and amazing by sending our brains positive messages. Our brains love mantras. The more often we tell our brains these positive messages, the happier and more confident we become. And the happier and more confident we are, the kinder we become. When this happens, we become the best versions of ourselves.

Now pick a mantra that you really liked. Say it over and over in your brain. Keep saying it over and over until you hear the sound of the singing bowl telling you to come back to the present moment.

Teaching Mindfulness for Brain and Heart Power

While there are many ways to become more mindful, cultivating positive intentional thoughts and strengthening compassionate hearts is the essence of Mindfulness. The practices in this section differ in that they welcome us to look internally at ourselves and the way we move through thoughts and emotions. At Challenge to Change, we call this Brain and Heart Power.

When we think of Brain Power, we often think of the mind functionally; focusing on a task, problem-solving, or its ability to recall memories and facts. While Mindfulness practices can strengthen this mechanical part of the brain, they can also encourage more positive thinking, assist with stress management skills, and promote overall better mental health.

Brain Power flexes the muscles of the mind by teaching us to watch our thoughts and emotions without judgment. Developing the habit of neutrally watching our thoughts gives us the ability to become more aware of limiting belief systems and negative self-talk that may have become second nature to us. When we become comfortable examining our negative beliefs, we can challenge their validity. This truly is a superpower because it gives us space to develop more compassionate and productive ways of thinking and being.

For example, perhaps one day you hurriedly send an email to your team at work before leaving for lunch. Hours later, you reread your email and notice that it contains a typo. Your natural assumption is that others noticed your mistake and now think less of your professional abilities because of it. You start to doubt your own intelligence and begin searching for signs that others doubt you too. This snowball effect causes you to view any future mistakes you make as a reason to question your own intellect.

If these thought patterns are left unchecked, the untrue thought, "I am stupid," can become ingrained in your mind. You may jokingly, or perhaps seriously, even say this out loud to a friend or spouse, further solidifying this unhealthy thought in your brain. Brain Power asks you to hear the untrue thought, "I am stupid," in your mind, and notice where it is coming from. Perhaps it developed from pressure you put on yourself to be perfect, or it came from something unkind someone said to you in the past.

Brain Power asks you to question the validity of your thinking. We know our intelligence is not measured by one email, and mistakes are simply an essential part of being human. It is unlikely that anyone's perception of you was drastically changed based upon one email. Once you recognize these truths, you can begin to offer yourself more compassionate dialogue, such as affirming that one can be smart and capable while still making mistakes. Sometimes a positive mantra, such as, "I am trying," can go far in helping to rebuild your confidence.

When initially learning about Brain Power practices, it is easy to become frustrated with ourselves for having negative thoughts and feelings. This is why it is imperative to strengthen Heart Power along with Brain Power simultaneously.

Heart Power practices help generate feelings of compassion, forgiveness, and love for one's self and others. When we build compassion for ourselves, it becomes easier to extend this same kindness to others in our lives, even those we do not know well or do not like very much.

Heart Power asks us to view ourselves, including our shortcomings, without judgment. While Brain Power provides insight to our thought patterns, Heart Power provides positive reframes to help ups consistently learn to think and live with kindness. Using these two concepts together gives us the opportunity to become happier, healthier, and kinder people, which leads to more positive social and emotional growth.

Building Brain and Heart Power in order to have a positive relationship with one's self is something people of all ages strive for. However, it is not something that is often explicitly taught. A great example of examining both simultaneously is the dynamic of our Inner Best Friend and our Inner Critic, a symbolic representation of the two voices that live within each one of us.

The voice we hear that cheers us on, reminds us of our strengths, and gives us positive affirmations is our Inner Best Friend. Conversely, the voice that tells us we are not good enough and we are doomed to fail is our Inner Critic. We especially love to use this exercise with children as they closely identify with the positive impact a best friend can have on our confidence and esteem.

It can be challenging for people of all ages to identify which voice has the metaphorical microphone in their minds. We have found one guiding question to be beneficial in determining who is speaking: "Would I talk to my best friend the same way I am thinking about myself?" If the answer is no, it is likely that the Inner Critic is holding the microphone in your mind. Brain and Heart Power remind us that we can hand the microphone to our Inner Best friend at any time without needing to judge ourselves for having an Inner Critic in our lives.

Learning to positively reframe our thoughts and examine the context of our emotions does not mean that we eliminate all negative thoughts and feelings from our lives altogether. We will all inevitably encounter uncomfortable events and circumstances that lead to negative thoughts and feelings. However, using Mindfulness for Brain and Heart Power guides us to be more intentional with the thoughts we allow to occupy space in our minds over extended periods of time. In this way, these practices help individuals cultivate an emotionally safe environment inside of themselves.

Explaining why these practices are important and creating honest dialogue around them make them much more meaningful. These exercises require a high level of trust, respect, and empathy. When teaching these practices, consider what you can appropriately share with others regarding your own thoughts, feelings, and experiences based on the topics at hand. It is very impactful for both children and adults to be aware that everyone struggles with negative thought patterns, self-judgment, and criticism over the course of their lives. Modeling how you apply these practices in your daily life can inspire others to create a positive shift in their own minds and hearts as well.

Just like any other muscle group in the body, the more we use the muscles of our brains for positive thinking and the muscles of our hearts for compassion, the stronger they become.

When we practice these exercises daily, we learn to rely on them like any other healthy habit in our lives. Strengthening our Brain and Heart Powers creates a ripple effect within ourselves and out into the world by increasing our capacity for love, kindness, and compassion.

Affirming Who You Are

To affirm something means to acknowledge it as fact. We sometimes affirm others simply to bring positivity into their lives; we can also offer affirmations to someone in order to give emotional support during uncertain times. This exercise does both.

Begin by introducing mantras. Explain that a mantra is a positive affirmation, typically composed of three words, beginning with, "I am," and ending with a positive phrase. Mantras can be used when we are doubting ourselves, such as when we are scared to do something, or any time we need to remind ourselves the truth of who we are.

Ask participants to choose positive affirmations for themselves. These can be something they know they are, or something that they wish to become. The only requirement for an affirmation is that it expresses something good about yourself.

Examples: I am brave, I am strong, I am kind, I am beautiful, I am smart, I am creative, I am compassionate, I am enough, I am joyful, I am worthy, I am patient.

Gather participants into a circle. The group will go around the circle with each individual sharing his or her positive affirmation one at time. After each person shares his or her mantra, the group responds with the words, "Yes, you are!" In this way, the group affirms for each individual that what they have said is true.

To enhance this Mindfulness experience, pass around a singing bowl and have each person play the bowl after sharing his or her affirmation.

Gratitude

To be grateful means to be thankful. People who practice gratitude often feel calmer and more peaceful because they recognize how full and complete their lives truly are; they don't feel the need to collect more and more "things" in order to feel happy.

It is important to practice expressing gratitude for what we have because it lets others know we appreciate what it is they bring into our lives. Expressing gratitude also helps us to have a positive outlook on ourselves.

Practicing gratitude has many benefits including strengthening the immune system, increasing optimism, improving sleep patterns, and decreasing stress levels. [32]

There are countless ways to practice gratitude with people of all ages. Below are three of Challenge to Change's favorite gratitude practices.

Gratitude Rampage

Ensure that participants have a basic understanding of what it means to be grateful, and then explain that a rampage is something that happens quickly or in a frenzy.

Round One: Give group members a few moments to think about, or write down, at least ten things they are grateful for. Partner individuals into pairs or trios or allow them to find their own partners. Instruct partners to face one another. The pair will ping-pong back and forth for one minute saying as many things as they can that they are grateful for.

After Round One, ask participants to notice what they all started doing—smiling. Thinking of things that make us happy actually makes us experience joy in the immediate moment.

Round Two: Participants share their gratitudes with their partners, but they must each offer something original. This means they cannot repeat something their partner has already said. For example, if the first partner says, "My mom," the second partner cannot say, "My mom," as well. Although the partners are likely referencing different mothers, having this rule in place requires that both individuals practice more active listening.

This can be repeated as many times as you would like. Feel free to add in challenges for each round with the possibility of reducing the time to thirty seconds.

Possible Challenges: Gratitudes that are larger than the size of the room; Gratitudes smaller than the palm of your hand; Gratitude for people; Gratitude for things you cannot see; Gratitude for things you can hear, etc.

Adaptation: Try this in a whole group setting by gathering the participants together in a circle. Time the group as they go around in the circle sharing what they are each grateful for. Do this for three rounds and see if the group can beat their best time each round. When participants are familiar with this practice, it can be a great way to start a class, end a class, or to shift the energy of the room when it is running too high or too low.

Gratitude Alphabet

Have participants brainstorm things they are grateful for associated with each letter of the alphabet. Individuals can begin by writing these lists in journals, and then sharing out loud round-robin style. The share begins with gratitudes that start with the letter **A**, and ends with those that start with the letter **Z**.

You could also choose to write the letters of the alphabet on a board in the center of the room and have the group brainstorm a gratitude item for each letter.

Alternatively, you could use this as an icebreaker activity in a group setting with each person saying something they are grateful for that starts with the first letter of their name. For example, "My name is Matt and I am grateful for macaroni."

Gratitude Jar

Start your own collection of gratitude by implementing a Gratitude Jar. This can be any jar, cup, or vase that you set aside for the purpose of collecting pieces of paper that contain your written gratitudes. A Gratitude Jar is a great addition to any home, office, classroom, or sports team.

To start the jar, ask your community to write down things for which they are grateful. This can be done intentionally or spontaneously. For example, if you work with the same individuals weekly, you might choose to have a "Feel Good Friday" ritual where participants each write something they are grateful for on a piece of paper and stick it in the jar every Friday afternoon. You might also encourage group members to write gratitudes and put them in the jar spontaneously when they see something great happening in the community.

Create the time and space to read these gratitudes aloud with others. Perhaps you choose to read them as a group bi-weekly, monthly, or at the end of the year.

Complimenting Your Community

For many people, it can be more challenging to receive a compliment than it is to give one. This activity asks for participants to give and receive compliments with a peer, and to give compliments to themselves.

This activity can be adapted for all ages. You may assign partners or allow participants to find their own. If you are working with younger children, consider having groups of five instead of pairs. This will allow you to circulate in the room to monitor and guide discussions more easily.

You may also choose to begin this activity with a whole-group demonstration. If doing so, ask for one volunteer to come to the center of a circle while the group goes around and says something nice about that individual. This can be a really great activity to do for individuals on their birthdays or to celebrate special accomplishments and contributions within the group setting.

To begin, give participants time to brainstorm one to three compliments they can give to their partners. If working with a group of five, allow group members adequate time to think of one compliment for each person in the group.

When the partners meet, have them face one another and encourage them to make eye contact as they share their compliments.

When this is finished, you may choose to ask participants to write down three compliments they have for themselves. Depending on their age, you can challenge them in this a bit by asking them to identify one physical, one mental, and one emotional characteristic of themselves that they admire. Let participants know recognizing positive attributes helps to build self-confidence.

Throw Away Your Stress
By Anne Funke

Stress is inevitable and should not be ignored. Sometimes stress can even be healthy when it pushes us to meet our goals and accomplishments in a positive manner. However, too often we let stress take over our lives without pausing to recognize what is at the root of the symptoms of our stress. This activity is intended for individuals ages ten and up.

Explain all of the steps for this activity before beginning. Participants will write down a current stress or a worry on a piece of scrap paper. Be sure individuals do not write their names on their papers. You might choose to offer some examples for them such as, "*I am worried I am not going to do well on the math test,*" *or*, "*I am stressed about a doctor's appointment tomorrow.*"

After individuals write down something that is stressful for them, the group will crumple their papers into little balls. Provide a countdown to prepare them to throw the balls into a designated area in the room. This should be a generally empty or clear space. Participants will then stand up, choose a piece of paper from the floor or designated area, and return to their seats. After reading the statement written on the page, each individual will write words of encouragement for the anonymous peer who wrote it. These responses should be thrown back into the circle with the exercise repeated two to three more times.

You may choose to read a few or all of these pages out loud to the group. You may also choose for participants to sift through the pages in order to find their original piece of paper with the added written words of encouragement.

Option to facilitate a conversation about what it feels like to receive and offer words of encouragement from a peer.

Positive Post-It® Project

This activity requires Post-it® Notes and is incredibly versatile. The intention behind this project is for group participants to create positive messages for themselves or for others. Incorporate this project into your Mindfulness curriculum as you see fit, making any adaptations needed to serve your students and accommodate the physical environment you are working in.

Option One: Give each participant one Post-It® Note to write a positive message for themselves. This can be in the form of a positive "I am" statement, a quote, a motivational message, or perhaps an inspirational drawing. Encourage individuals to place this Post-it® Note somewhere they will see it daily; in their planners, in their cars, on their bathroom mirrors, on their computers, or next to their beds.

Option Two: Assign a person to each group member for whom they will create a positive Post-it® Note. These notes can contain any uplifting message or image they can think of for their partners. Participants will anonymously leave these messages for their partners to find at a designated time.

Option Three: If doing this activity in a school, students create anonymous positive Post-it® Notes for community members to find. These can be placed on lockers, on a hallway bulletin board, or in a community space such as the library or cafeteria. If pursuing this option, be sure to check with your administration and or custodial staff before posting these messages.

Conclusion

As we come to the end of our journey together, we'd like to thank you for taking the time to put your phone down and put your feet up so that you could explore the world of Mindfulness with us. Mindfulness truly is one of the most powerful personal tools we have at our disposal; it is always readily available wherever and whenever we need it, and it doesn't cost a thing. Moreover, when we make the effort to live more mindfully, we gain important insight, act with more intention, and are able to live more purposeful lives.

Throughout the pages of this book, we strove to bring you real and practical knowledge as to how you can slow down your busy life in order to practice Mindfulness. Our goal was to show you how to connect with your mind, body, and breath so that you can get to know yourself on a deeper level. We also wanted to give you insight as to why practicing Mindfulness is so important not only for you, but for the children in your life as well.

Although there are multiple paths that one can take toward living more mindfully, at the center of the journey there is always The Pause. Learning to give yourself space to reflect on your thoughts and feelings before taking action is the heart and soul of Mindfulness. It is what every Mindfulness practice is building towards, and we encourage you to practice The Pause with intention so that it becomes a natural reaction in your day-to-day life.

It is also important to remember that Mindfulness is a way of living that doesn't require a complete lifestyle makeover in order to be effective. A little bit of Mindfulness truly goes a long way. We have introduced you to the five ways we teach Mindfulness at Challenge to Change—breath practices, physical movement, sensory experiences, meditation, and activities that speak to the brain and heart—and we encourage you to simply try one or two exercises a day. Then take the time to notice. Notice the changes between your actions and reactions. What is different? How do you feel? Then ask: "What is next for me? Where do I want my Mindfulness journey to go?"

We would love to hear how these practices have affected you. Please contact us through our website, www.challengetochangeinc.com. Hearing witness as to how Mindfulness has changed others' worlds for the better gives inspiration to our mindful journeys as well.

Now go out and change the world. YOU are a change-maker who has the ability in your mind and the passion in your heart to make the world a better, more peaceful place for the people who are here now and for the future generations that are yet to come.

Namaste.

Yoga Poses

BUTTERFLY POSE

CHILD'S POSE

COBRA

DOWNWARD
FACING DOG

FORWARD FOLD

MOUNTAIN POSE

PLANK

REVERSE WARRIOR

SEATED FORWARD
FOLD

TREE POSE

UPWARD FACING
DOG

WARRIOR I

WARRIOR II

With Gratitude

We are thankful for all of the roads in life—both bumpy and smooth—that led us as individuals to the practice of Mindfulness. We are fortunate because it was on this journey that our paths crossed. For the road that we have traveled together as a team at Challenge to Change we are especially thankful.

We are filled with gratitude for every situation that had to transpire for this book to come to life.

Challenges like death, divorce, sobriety, and loss have been some of our greatest teachers and the catalysts of change that allowed us to grow into the women we are today. Each of these experiences has been the mud for our lotus; and for that we are blessed.

Thank you to the year 2020. Without you, we would not have been forced to pause for so long, giving us time to turn inward. It was during this mindful journey into ourselves that we recognized we could share our teachings in a different way—through literature. And thank you to the television show *Friends*, for giving us a reference point for this whole year. PIVOT!

Thank you to all of our teachers who ignited a spark in us to become educators ourselves; whether in a yoga studio, a school classroom, or in our own homes. It was great teachers in our own lives who inspired us to share our passions with others.

To the first sets of eyes on our book: Dale S., Lynnea C., Barb H., Barb O., Linda G., and Dolly C.— Thank you! You saw this book in its most vulnerable stages and helped us build it into the best version we could. In doing so, you helped support us in sharing Mindfulness with others.

An incredibly heart-felt thank you to everyone who "Down Dogs" with us on our yoga mats whether in the studio or through virtual offerings. We honor all of the schools that participate in our programming; especially the educators and students involved in our Yoga and Mindfulness in the Schools project. You are the heartbeat behind what we do.

We do not have enough expressions of gratitude for our team of change-makers at Challenge to Change. Each one of you makes who we are and what we do better, stronger, and more beautiful. You are such a light in this world.

Mostly, we want to thank our friends and families who supported us in the creation of *Grow*. You have rallied behind us through every step of this journey. Thank you for helping us move beyond moments of frustration, for keeping us inspired, and for listening to us when this book was all we talked about for nine months. WE DID IT! (Insert happy dance).

Thank you. Thank you. Thank you.

Sources Cited

[1] Willard, Christopher. (2010). *Child's Mind: Mindfulness Practices to Help Our Children Be More Focused, Calm, and Relaxed*. Parallax Press.

[2] Kabat-Zinn, Jon. (2005). *Wherever You Go, There You Are: Mindfulness Meditation in Everyday Life*. Hachette Books.

[3] Tzu, Lao. (1989). *Tao Te Ching*. Vintage Press.

[4] James, Matt (2016, September 1) *React vs. Respond: What's the Difference?* https://www.psychologytoday.com/us/blog/focus-forgiveness/201609/react-vs-respond#:~:text=A%20reaction%20is%20survival%2Doriented,conscious%20mind%20and%20unconscious%20mind.

[5] Siegel, Daniel J. & Bryson, Tina Payne. (2019). *The Yes Brain: How to Cultivate Courage, Curiosity, and Resilience in Your Child*. Bantam Books.

[6] Mendel, B., Garner, S., Korlo, T., Bosia, S., & Pretsch, L. (2021). *Mindworks*. https://mindworks.org/.

[7] Puddicombe, Andy. (2010) *Headspace*. https://www.headspace.com/meditation/techniques.

[8] Welch, Ashley. (2019, May 1). *A Guide to 7 Different Types of Meditation*. https://www.everydayhealth.com/meditation/types/.

[9] Bertone, Holly J. (2020, October 2) *Which Meditation Type is Right For Me?* https://www.healthline.com/health/mental-health/types-of-meditation.

[10] Hyde, Melissa. (2020, May 19). *What is Sound Healing Meditation?* https://www.challengetochangeinc.com/post/what-is-sound-healing-meditation.

[11] Call, Annie Payson. (2007) *Nerves and Common Sense*. Book Jungle.

[12] Herrington, Sarah. (2014) *Essential Yoga*. Sweet Water Press.

[13] Lucas, Lucy. (2019) *Little Book of Yoga*. Gaia Books.

[14] Romine, Stepfanie. (2018, May 18). *Types of Yoga: A Guide to the Different Styles*. https://yogamedicine.com/guide-types-yoga-styles/.

[15] UpRising UK. (2016, July 20). *The Science Behind Mindfulness Meditation*. https://www.youtube.com/watch?v=VTAOj8FfCvs

[16] Korevaar, Dianna. & Downing, Liv. (2015, February 2). *Mind the Bump-Mindfulness and How the Brain Works*. https://www.youtube.com/watch?v=aNCB1MZDgQA.

[17] National Institute of Neurological Disorders and Stroke. (2020, February 13). *Brain Basics: Know Your Brain*. https://www.ninds.nih.gov/Disorders/Patient-Caregiver-Education/Know-Your-Brain.

[18] Dubuc, Brian. (2002) *The Evolutionary Layers of the Human Brain.* https://thebrain.mcgill.ca/flash/d/d_05/d_05_cr/d_05_cr_her/.

[19] Taren, A, Cresswell, D., Gianaros, P. (2013, May 22). *Dispositional Mindfulness Co-Varies with Smaller Amygdala and Caudate Volumes in Community Adults.* https://journals.plos.org/plosone/article?id=10.1371/journal.pone.0064574

[20] Borba, Michele. (2016). *Unselfie: Why Empathetic Kids Succeed in Our All-About-Me World.* Touchstone Press.

[21] Larson, Jennifer. (2020, June 22). *What to Know About Gamma Brain Waves.* https://www.healthline.com/health/gamma-brain-waves#benefits.

[22] World Health Organization. (2020, September 28). *Adolescent Mental Health.* https://www.who.int/news-room/fact-sheets/detail/adolescent-mental-health.

[23] Davis, Daphne M. and Hayes, Jeffrey A. (2012 July/August) *What are the Benefits of Mindfulness?.* American Psychological Association. Page 64. https://www.apa.org/monitor/2012/07-08/ce-corner.

[24] Harvard Health. *Benefits of Mindfulness: Practices for Improving Emotional and Physical Well-Being.* https://www.helpguide.org/harvard/benefits-of-mindfulness.htm#:~:text=Mindfulness%20improves%20physical%20health.&text=Mindfulness%20can%3A%20help%20relieve%20stress,sleep%2C%20and%20alleviate%20gastrointestinal%20difficulties.

[25] Suttie, Julie. (2018, October 29) *Five Science-Backed Reasons Mindfulness Meditation is Good for You.* https://www.mindful.org/five-ways-mindfulness-meditation-is-good-for-your-health/.

[26] Janz, P., Dawe, S., Wyllie, M. (2019, September 10). *Mindfulness-Based Program Embedded Within the Existing Curriculum Improves Executive Functioning and Behavior in Your Children: A Waitlist Controlled Trial.* https://www.ncbi.nlm.nih.gov/pmc/articles/PMC6746974/.

[27] Black, David S. & Fernando, Randima. (2013, June 19). *Mindfulness Training and Classroom Behavior Among Lower-Income and Ethnic Minority Elementary School Children.* Journal of Child and Family Studies. 1242-1246. https://www.ncbi.nlm.nih.gov/pmc/articles/PMC4304073/.

[28] Harvard Health Publishing. (2020, July 6). *Relaxation Techniques: Breath Control Helps Quell Errant Stress Response.* https://www.health.harvard.edu/mind-and-mood/relaxation-techniques-breath-control-helps-quell-errant-stress-response.

[29] Healthy Children. (2016). *Just Breathe: The Importance of Meditation Breaks for Children.* https://www.healthychildren.org/English/

healthy-living/emotional-wellness/Pages/Just-Breathe-The-Importance-of-Meditation-Breaks-for-Kids.aspx.

[30] Laskowski, Edward R (2020, April 21). *What are the Risks of Sitting Too Much?* https://www.mayoclinic.org/healthy-lifestyle/adult-health/expert-answers/sitting/faq-20058005.

[31] Willey, Kira. "Dance for the Sun". *Dance for the Sun: Yoga Songs for Kids*. Discmakers, 2006. CD.

[32] Morin, Amy. (2015, April 3). *7 Scientifically Proven Benefits of Gratitude.* https://www.psychologytoday.com/us/blog/what-mentally-strong-people-dont-do/201504/7-scientifically-proven-benefits-gratitude.

About the Authors

Although the words of this text were penned by three women, true authorship of <u>Grow</u> belongs to the team of change-makers who cowrote the story of Challenge to Change. Just like the lotus flower, Molly began her mission to bring mindfulness to others with the small seed of an idea. It took root through the support of others, and has since blossomed through the love and hard work that every team member at Challenge to Change has poured from their heart.

Thank you to each and every change-maker who helped write our story. This book belongs to you.

Julie Strittmatter

Julie lives each day committed to spreading the mission of Mindfulness, beginning with herself. Practicing Mindfulness in early adulthood had such a profound impact on Julie's life that she pursued her yoga instructor certification early in her career, as well as a degree in Secondary Education. Julie believes Mindfulness is for everyone, and she is grateful to be able to share these practices with people of all ages. Julie is an E-RYT 200, Registered Children's Yoga Teacher, and holds a degree in Secondary Education English from Slippery Rock University. Julie loves finding ways to weave her passion for Mindfulness into the educational system and has been successful in doing this with her own classroom in traditional schools, working with at-risk teens though wilderness therapy, and offering Mindfulness sessions for educators. Julie has dedicated most of her career to working with teens and was given the honor of Teacher of the Year by De-Witt, Iowa community schools in 2017. She is currently a content creator for Challenge to Change Inc. and owner of Sun + Soul Shine Yoga. Outside of the classroom and yoga studio, a deep love of travel, hiking, music, writing, and cooking fuels Julie's life adventures.

Melissa Hyde

Melissa Hyde is dedicated to social-emotional education in schools. A native of Los Angeles, California, Melissa received her Master of Arts in Education from Pepperdine University, then proceeded to work in a series of local schools that embraced collaborative learning, community-building, and early implementation of social-emotional standards. Melissa discovered yoga during her undergraduate years at the University of Iowa, and now works with Challenge to Change to bring yoga to children and teachers to help promote self-confidence and healthy emotional regulation skills. Melissa brings her love of writing to Challenge to Change as their Educational Staff Writer, as well as regularly contributing to several other publications in her local area. When not practicing yoga, writing, or teaching, Melissa spends time longing for the warm weather of California and cuddling with her fur babies—Banner, a gentle standard poodle, and Skye, a very fluffy and sassy cat.

Molly Schreiber

Molly Schreiber is the owner and founder of Challenge to Change Inc. in Dubuque, Iowa, a children's yoga studio offering lifelong wellness skills for people all of ages through the practices of fitness, yoga, meditation, and daily Mindfulness practices. As a former elementary teacher, working with students and school personnel is at the heart of Molly's mission. She believes that we can change the world by empowering children with skills that foster positive thinking and compassion for self and others. This belief inspired Molly to design various programming such as The Yoga in the Schools Project, Kids and Adult Yoga Teacher Trainings, online learning resources for school and families, numerous children's books, and countless other Mindfulness resources. Molly is an E-RYT 500, Registered Children's Yoga Teacher, and holds a Master's Degree from Western Illinois University in Education. She is a mother of four beautiful children: Sydney, Maggie, Jacob, and Maria, and wife to Tom. Regardless of the role she is in—mother, business owner, wife, friend, or teacher—Molly joyously shares her mission for helping people of all ages cultivate happy and healthy lifestyles.

Continue Growing

For more Mindfulness practices designed for children and teens, check out *A Classroom in Balance* also by Challenge to Change.

A Classroom in Balance is a perfect read for anyone looking to push "pause" in the lives of our youth using the power of Mindfulness. This fantastic resource shares one hundred scripted lessons and practices that can take place in ten minutes or less. This book suits both experienced Mindfulness practitioners and novices as it provides an overview of Mindfulness while offering practical and purposeful ways to teach it to others.

Through exercises such as journaling, meditation, mindful movements, and class discussions, this book benefits both the facilitator and practitioner by tending to the physical, mental, and emotional well-being of all who participate. Although originally intended for secondary education classroom teachers, these exercises are a wonderful addition to learning at any age. This is an invaluable resource for teachers, parents, counselors, youth group-leaders and coaches alike. Are you ready to create your own Classroom in Balance?

Grow with Challenge to Change

Challenge to Change Inc. offers signature Mindfulness programming for all ages. As a former educator, Molly Schreiber, founder and owner of Challenge to Change, keeps teachers and learners of all ages at the heart of her mission. Therefore, much of Challenge to Change's programming and resources were designed to support the happiness and health of children, teens, parents, and teachers. Located in Dubuque, Iowa, Challenge to Change spreads its mission far and wide through the use of virtual yoga classes, online training sessions, literature, and online resources.

Visit **challengetochangeinc.com** to see how our resources, trainings, and programs can support you on your Mindfulness journey!

RESOURCES

Our easy-to-use Yoga and Mindfulness resources were developed for use in a classroom, studio, or home setting.

Change The Station In Your Brain

CONTINUING EDUCATION

These courses were designed to help classroom teachers find ways to meaningfully integrate Mindfulness within the school day in a way that best serves their students and accommodates their scheduling needs.

TRAININGS

Our 95 hour, 200 hour, and 300 hour yoga teacher training programs empower teachers, parents, and yogis alike to share the practices of yoga and Mindfulness with toddlers, kids, teens, and adults.

PROGRAMMING

Challenge to Change's most popular program is The Yoga in the Schools Project, which provides meaningful thirty-minute lessons that support the social-emotional growth of students. Our mission offers in-person lessons locally around Dubuque, IA, as well as virtual programming for our more distant learning communities.

CLASSES AND WORKSHOPS

We are always exploring new ways to share yoga, Mindfulness, and meditation practices with others. Join us for an in-person or virtual class or workshop. We offer sound healing, family yoga, personalized yoga classes, children's camps, yoga birthday parties, and more.

Learn more about our mission, meet the team, and ignite your own Challenge to Change!

CPSIA information can be obtained
at www.ICGtesting.com
Printed in the USA
LVHW081523210821
695819LV00002B/253